IF I COULD ASK GOD
ONE
QUESTION

GREG JOHNSON

BETHANY HOUSE PUBLISHERS
MINNEAPOLIS, MINNESOTA 55438

If I Could Ask God One Question
Copyright © 1998
Greg Johnson

Tyndale House Publishers originally published a 1991 edition of this work by the same title. Many of these selections form the basis for the "I Wonder" notes in the *Life Application Bible for Students* from Tyndale.

Cover design by the Lookout Design Group

Published by Bethany House Publishers
A Ministry of Bethany Fellowship International
11400 Hampshire Avenue South
Bloomington, Minnesota 55438
www.bethanyhouse.com

Printed in the United States of America by
Bethany Press International, Bloomington, Minnesota 55438

Library of Congress Cataloging-in-Publication Data

Johnson, Greg, 1956–
    If I could ask God one question—/ by Greg Johnson.
      p. cm.
    Summary: Provides answers to some questions that teenagers commonly ask about God and the Christian faith.
    ISBN 0-7642-2093-4 (pbk.)
    1. Teenagers—Religious life—Miscellanea. 2. Christian life— Miscellanea—Juvenile literature. 3. Theology, Doctrinal— Miscellanea—Juvenile literature. [1. Christian life.] I. Title.
BV4531.2.J58   1998
248.8'3—dc21

                                                      97–45478
                                                       CIP
                                                       AC

BHP BOOKS BY GREG JOHNSON

If I Could Ask God One Question

WITH SUSIE SHELLENBERGER

Camp, Car Washes, Heaven, and Hell

Cars, Curfews, Parties, and Parents

Life, Love, Music, and Money

Lockers, Lunch Lines, Chemistry, and Cliques

GREG JOHNSON is the former editor of *Breakaway* magazine for teen boys and author of twenty-one books. A graduate of Northwest Christian College, Greg has been involved with teens for more than twenty years and has worked with Youth for Christ and Focus on the Family. He and his wife have two sons and make their home in Colorado Springs.

INTRODUCTION

As a Christian of more than twenty years, I've never been afraid to ask God the tough questions. If a thought went through my brain that didn't have an immediate answer, I was persistent until I found one. Thankfully, when I first became a Christian, I was taught well. Christian friends always pointed me back to the Bible for the answers I sought.

When I was first starting out in the faith, I naturally asked God a lot of irrelevant questions the Bible never intended to answer. But for ninety-five percent of the *important* questions I asked, God's Word was always there, ready and waiting to give me the truth. The other five percent? I'll have to wait for heaven. In this life, they're unanswerable. But that's okay.

Perhaps you're a brand-new Christian who's starting from scratch. The Bible looks like a big book with no pictures, and living the Christian life is . . . well . . . something too confusing to think about. If that is the case, this book is for you.

Or maybe you've grown up in the church and suddenly are asking the whys and hows to a faith that's becoming your own and is sometimes tough to grow into. The Scriptures and illustrations used in this book will hopefully cause your faith to be brought into clearer focus.

Either way, for as long as you live, God's not intimidated by *anything*—least of all, honest feelings and questions asked from a heart genuinely looking for an answer. Since we can't intimidate or surprise him, and since he's not going to make us look stupid if we ask a dumb question, then maybe we should realize how approachable he truly is.

I wrote the first edition of this work in 1991. In the back of the book I left an address where people could write if they didn't find the answers they were looking for. I received more than two hundred letters with more questions, honest questions . . . tough questions! Many of my answers to these people are included in this new edition.

What I've learned as I continue to stumble my way through the Christian life is that God most enjoys progress in his kids. When I move from point A to point B, as I'm heading to point Z, I've made progress, and God is pleased.

The pages following are designed to aid in your progress toward the goal of understanding the Bible and loving God with all your heart, your soul, and your *mind*.

The questions and answers in this book have come from three sources: fifteen years of working with teenagers, five years as editor of *Breakaway* magazine, and the Bible. Though some of the questions are tough, I hope the answers are simple.

Being a Christian wasn't intended to be a *religion* that only a few could figure out, but a *relationship* based on trust. Though Jesus loves the intellectual who "has to know," he especially delights in believers who simply want to be with him. As you seek the answers to your questions, realize this: There's no greater joy than simply being with Jesus the Christ and allowing his Word to remind you that he loves you deeply, each new day.

Greg Johnson
Colorado Springs

So many things try to crowd God out of my life.
I've got school, homework, volleyball, and a job
at Burger King. Even church activities keep me
busy. How much of me does God want?

1 SAMUEL 8:4-9

So all the elders of Israel gathered together and came to
Samuel at Ramah. They said to him, "You are old, and your sons do
not walk in your ways; now appoint a king to lead us, such as all the
other nations have."

But when they said, "Give us a king to lead us," this
displeased Samuel; so he prayed to the Lord. And the Lord told him:
"Listen to all that the people are saying to you; it is not you they
have rejected as their king, but me. As they have done from the day I
brought them up out of Egypt until this day, forsaking me and
serving other gods, so they are doing to you. Now listen to them; but
warn them solemnly and let them know what the king who will reign
over them will do."

The answer is, he wants all of you. God does not want to
be just another addition to your life—he wants everything
you do to revolve around him!

Bike tires are only as strong as the hub of the wheel. If a
tire were made up only of rim and spokes, the wheel would
soon collapse under the constant pounding and pressure.

The spokes in our lives are those things you mentioned that are important to us, like family, friends, school, sports, or entertainment. If our life revolves around any one of these "spokes," eventually the constant pounding and pressures of our world will wear us down and possibly cause us to collapse.

God knows this and has provided the strong center that will hold us together. By ignoring God and trying to run our own lives, we will be living as though we believe the spokes are strong enough to carry us.

For centuries the Jewish people complained to God and asked him for a king to rule over them. What they were actually saying was, "God, since we can't see you, we can't trust you to take care of us. Give us someone we can see who will rule over us." Eventually God gave in to their request. The results, however, were devastating. Because they put their focus on what a man could do for them (a weak "spoke"), their enemies soon overpowered the entire nation until all of the people of Israel were forced to live away from the Promised Land.

The Old Testament graphically describes what happened when God's people rejected him from being their leader (the hub). Jesus Christ should be the hub of our lives. This means that we should consult him and his Word first.

Let me first talk about formal times with God. Really, the only way to stay consistent is accountability. That is, having someone ask you about how it's going. Without those gentle reminders, we simply forget or it gets pushed aside. Can your mom do that in a gentle way? I'm sure she doesn't need something else to remind you about, but it might even help her, too. Maybe you could challenge each other. If not her, how about the wife of your youth leader, or one of the female sponsors at your church? Maybe there's a close friend who has the same struggle.

I've had the most success by placing my formal time of Bible reading and prayer between two things I do every day: shower and breakfast, or breakfast and leaving for work.

But there's a bigger question here. Does God just want

five or ten minutes of our day, or does he want us to think about him and talk with him throughout the day?

God wants my whole day, not a small portion. I've come to realize that spending ten minutes with God does not make me spiritual. Though it's essential that Christians do this, it's just as important that we recognize him all day. It's not as hard as it might seem. I find myself thanking him all day long, asking him for help on things, or just remembering that the God who made the whole universe lives inside me. It's revolutionized my relationship with him. I really have felt that he is with me.

When things begin to crowd out your relationship with God, try writing down all of your priorities. Ask a trusted Christian friend if any one of these "spokes" is taking the place of God in your life.

CHAPTER 2

I've been a Christian for about two months, and I feel so far behind spiritually, especially compared to friends who have been Christians for a lot longer. Sometimes it gets pretty discouraging. They know all of the right words, they pray better, and they can find things in their Bible. How do I catch up?

COLOSSIANS 2:6–7

So then, just as you received Christ Jesus as Lord, continue to live in him, rooted and built up in him, strengthened in the faith as you were taught, and overflowing with thankfulness.

We live in a world that makes it nearly impossible not to compare ourselves with others. Whether it's looks, clothes, athletic abilities, or other talents, it seems everyone's goal is to be up to, or beyond, someone else's level.

Sometimes we even compare our life as a Christian to others'. You must, however, fight this urge and recognize two essential facts.

First, receiving forgiveness for our sin and asking Christ to come into our life is like having a seed planted in our heart (see 1 Corinthians 3:6). Any seed planted must first take root before it grows and blossoms.

Do you remember in first grade when you planted a seed in a clear plastic cup? If the seed was planted close enough to the edge, you would see that the roots would grow downward first; then a few days later a plant would appear above the dirt. It was miraculous!

The only difference between you and your friends is that they have had more time to spread their roots down deep. They've lived longer in "vital union with him" and have "drawn up nourishment from him" for a longer period of time.

When you took the first step of faith to trust Christ with your life, that was like the seed being planted. From that point on it's up to *you* and *God* to nourish the seed.

Rooting your new relationship with Christ nourishes your faith. This means getting to know God better through reading and obeying his Word—the Bible (see Romans 10:17).

Second, God doesn't compare one Christian to another. So don't you try. That would be like a father wanting his two-year-old son to throw a baseball as well as his nine-year-old. He can't.

As Christians, we never get to a point where we have reached perfection and are totally mature. But our love and appreciation for God can always grow deeper as he shows us new areas in our lives to trust him with.

Enjoy these beginning stages of your faith by taking in all of the spiritual nourishment you can handle. Remember, the stronger and deeper your roots grow below the surface, the more beautiful and fruitful you will be as a Christian (see John 15:4–5).

CHAPTER 3

Since becoming a Christian, it seems like I'm always fighting certain thoughts and habits that I used to never give a second thought.

ROMANS 7:15–21

I don't understand myself at all, for I really want to do what is right, but I can't. I do what I don't want to—what I hate. I know perfectly well that what I am doing is wrong, and my bad conscience proves that I agree with these laws I am breaking. But I can't help myself, because I'm no longer doing it. It is sin inside me that is stronger than I am that makes me do these evil things.

I know I am rotten through and through, so far as my old sinful nature is concerned. No matter which way I turn I can't make myself do right. I want to but I can't. When I want to do good, I don't; and when I try not to do wrong, I do it anyway. Now if I am doing what I don't want to, it is plain where the trouble is: sin still has me in its evil grasp.

It seems to be a fact of life that when I want to do what is right, I inevitably do what is wrong.

Picture your life as a door. Before you became a Christian, your sins were like nails pounded into the door and left there. When you asked Christ to forgive you, all of the nails you'd collected were removed. Unfortunately, what was left was a door full of holes, not very pleasant to look at and not very useful.

But God began patching up the holes. More accurately, he began to heal the scars left by sin, so the door looked unscarred even after years of constant pounding. We can truly become a new creation (see 2 Corinthians 5:17).

That's why it's so important for people to come to know Christ's forgiveness early in life. Because we inherited a sinful nature from Adam (Romans 5:12), time and wrong choices can pound some pretty large nails into our lives. And those scars may take longer to heal.

What you're experiencing is a new sensitivity to sin. Since sin wants to "drive a hole" in you, and Christ wants to keep you unscarred by the effects of sin, it's no longer comfortable to ignore the constant pounding. Confessing your sin, I hope you're aware, will always remove the nail (see 1 John 1:9).

This new sensitivity to sin means two things. First, it's a definite sign that God's Holy Spirit has truly entered your life (Romans 8:9). It's likely you would still be numb to the nails (sin) if you had rejected Christ's forgiveness.

Second, it means that God is reminding you of his great love (Romans 8:38–39). God is now using your conscience to advise you where you could stray off course. He doesn't want you to be left scarred by the consequences of your sin, so he begins at the source of it—your thought life.

I like the idea about having a personal faith in God. What I don't like is having to go to church with a bunch of older people. Why can't there be a church with just kids my own age?

HEBREWS 10:23–25

Let us hold unswervingly to the hope we profess, for he who promised is faithful. And let us consider how we may spur one another on toward love and good deeds. Let us not give up meeting together, as some are in the habit of doing, but let us encourage one another—and all the more as you see the Day approaching.

Imagine growing up without a family. It's tough to think of life without at least one parent who really cares.

Now imagine growing up with just brothers and sisters in the house and no parents at all. For a day or two it may seem like heaven, but very soon you'd see its chaos. Eventually you'd miss having someone to take care of your basic needs like laundry, meals, cable and phone bills, perhaps an occasional hug or listening ear.

Families are designed to take care of your daily needs and to give you the continual love and guidance you need as you're growing up. Plus, because they have been around longer, your mom or dad often know what to do when a tough circumstance comes up (as much as you may hate to admit it).

Jude 21 says to "stay always within the boundaries where God's love can reach and bless you" (TLB).

Church is our spiritual family that provides that safe boundary where God's love can reach us. If we stay away, we're left to try to survive by ourselves. If all we had around were other kids, church would be like a house with no adults. Pretty soon we'd recognize that many of our needs were not getting met.

The church, like the family, can often be underappreciated for the role it plays in our spiritual growth. Some Christians don't recognize its influence until years later, when they realize they'd still be spiritual babies without the church's influence and love.

Many years ago I entered a ministry where I had to raise my own support. God had laid it upon my heart to reach non-Christian teens and provided an organization to work with to accomplish this important mission. I'd only been in my home church a few years when God put this call on my life, so I didn't know how they'd respond. The church was more traditional, and it had a lot of old people whom I didn't know. But when the pastor told the congregation I was giving my life to the ministry, people came from everywhere to support my ministry faithfully for years. Many became my very best friends. They prayed, they gave, they sent encouraging letters.

The point is, God uses the local church family in ways you won't believe. He knows what your needs are not only today but also in the future. If you're plugged into a church, then God has a way to meet your needs.

CHAPTER 5

Prayer is confusing. With so many things out
there that I want and so many things I know I
need, how do I know what to ask God for?

1 KINGS 3:3–13

*Solomon showed his love for the Lord by walking according to
the statutes of his father David, except that he offered sacrifices and
burned incense on the high places.*

*The king went to Gibeon to offer sacrifices, for that was the
most important high place, and Solomon offered a thousand burnt
offerings on that altar. At Gibeon the Lord appeared to Solomon
during the night in a dream, and God said, "Ask for whatever you
want me to give you."*

*Solomon answered, "You have shown great kindness to your
servant, my father David, because he was faithful to you and
righteous and upright in heart. You have continued this great
kindness to him and have given him a son to sit on his throne this
very day.*

*"Now, O Lord my God, you have made your servant king in
place of my father David. But I am only a little child and do not
know how to carry out my duties. Your servant is here among the
people you have chosen, a great people, too numerous to count or
number. So give your servant a discerning heart to govern your people*

and to distinguish between right and wrong. For who is able to govern this great people of yours?"

The Lord was pleased that Solomon had asked for this. So God said to him, "Since you have asked for this and not for a long life or wealth for yourself, nor have asked for the death of your enemies but for discernment in administering justice, I will do what you have asked. I will give you a wise and discerning heart, so that there will never have been anyone like you, nor will there ever be. Moreover, I will give you what you have not asked for—both riches and honor—so that in your lifetime you will have no equal among kings."

Do you realize your mom is faced with the same question every time she goes to the grocery store? She knows what you *want* to eat, but she buys (mostly) what you *need* to eat. Her experience as a "home engineer" keeps you healthy!

God also wants you to be healthy. He knows exactly what to give you and when to give it to you. Jesus said, "Which of you, if his son asks for bread, will give him a stone? Or if he asks for a fish, will give him a snake? If you, then, though you are evil, know how to give good gifts to your children, how much more will your Father in heaven give good gifts to those who ask him!" (Matthew 7:9–11).

Your mother was probably very glad when you asked for an apple for a snack instead of ice cream (has that day come?). It shows that you're becoming aware of what it will take to keep yourself healthy. Though ice cream tastes better, apples are far better for you.

Our requests to God can sometimes be very selfish, centered only on what we want and not on what we need. God the Father longs for the day when we ask him for what we really need or, better yet, what others need.

Solomon had the privilege of asking for anything he wanted from God. Of all of the choices available to him, Solomon made the one that was most pleasing to God. He asked for wisdom. God responded by giving Solomon more wisdom than any other man, and God gave him riches and honor, as well, so that others could benefit from the wisdom God gave him.

Selfish prayers are rarely answered yes by God because he loves us too much. Although a child whines for candy an hour before dinner, a wise parent will always say no.

The best things to pray for are those that will ultimately help other people. A perfect example is to ask for the health of someone who is sick. While it's not God's will to heal everyone immediately, God is still in the business of healing body and soul.

When you pray for yourself, a few good examples of what to ask for are character qualities (such as patience, self-control, gentleness) that will help you get along better with other people and will point others toward Christ. God cares about immediate requests, as well. Tests, athletic events, guy/girl stuff, all are good requests to take to the Lord.

When you have needs, you should never be afraid to ask God to meet them. He loves to answer the prayers of his children!

CHAPTER 6

Before I became a Christian, I used to read the newspaper horoscopes. Is there anything wrong with this, or is it just harmless fun? And all of my friends believe in UFOs. What does the Bible say about life on other planets?

DEUTERONOMY 18:9–13

When you enter the land the Lord your God is giving you, do not learn to imitate the detestable ways of the nations there. Let no one be found among you who sacrifices his son or daughter in the fire, who practices divination or sorcery, interprets omens, engages in witchcraft, or casts spells, or who is a medium or spiritist or who consults the dead. Anyone who does these things is detestable to the Lord and because of these detestable practices the Lord your God will drive out those nations before you. You must be blameless before the Lord your God.

The Bible is pretty open about how bad horoscopes are. They are tools Satan uses to get people distracted from allowing God to lead their lives. Look in a Bible concordance under "divination and witchcraft" and you'll see what God says about it.

Unfortunately, because they're in newspapers and at the checkout stands, many think that they're harmless. A poll taken not long ago found that sixty percent of thirteen- to fifteen-year-olds believed in astrology. And it wasn't a girl thing, either. Forty-three percent were guys. Worse yet, there was no difference between church-going teens and those who didn't attend!

With those percentages just among teens, it's obvious astrology is *big* business. The attraction to astrology is that it instructs people on matters of the soul without being morally demanding. Convenient, huh? In an age when people have effectively rid themselves of Christian influence because of God's "demands," astrology can be very attractive.

Where did it come from and what's the goal? How real is it?

The ancient Greeks named each planet in our solar system after the mythical gods they worshiped. All of their gods had distinct, well-developed personalities that set them apart from others.

Astrology makes predictions about the future based on your birth, where you were born, and how the stars and planets (the characteristics of the gods) line up with one another. Astrologers give these predictions to you in three ways.

The first is newspaper and grocery store astrologies called *speculations*. They use ambiguous language and never give specific disclosures. The goal is to hook unsuspecting readers into believing the predictions so that they'll want to read more. A discerning mind can quickly realize anyone could write these blurbs without knowledge of the planets and probably say something that matches a person's situation as often as the "real" horoscope does. But for the unsuspecting, they can be very enticing.

Generalizations, the second stage, give more specific information about future or current events based on more detailed information. They are usually found in books on astrology in the New Age section of bookstores or libraries. The problem is each author offers a different interpretation based on the same astrological patterns.

Finally, those who have swallowed the circumstantial, partial truths of astrology are in danger of delving into the *self-disclosure* stage. This is when you actually consult an expert one-on-one.

People easily fall into this stage because both astrologer and client are trained to think *planet* instead of mythical god. Therefore, they talk *planet* instead of religion. It's hard to prove whether the name change is intentional or calculated, but it is a deception.

How do people get hooked? Everyone starts in stage one! Astrology is one hundred percent based on imagined stories of imagined gods. It is, in the fullest sense, gaining advice from ancient gods of a peculiar polytheistic religion.

Many Christians, however, would say the gods are actually demon-inspired and may have been the characteristics of demons themselves. The implications behind this belief are all too obvious. Most would agree there is power behind this false religion, but it's deceptive and potentially destructive. I would strongly recommend that if you are in the habit of checking out your horoscope in the newspaper—stop.

You also asked about UFOs. The Bible says nothing about them, so it is open for debate. Personally, I do not think they exist. I feel the enemy is using them to distract people from the love of God. By throwing something "sensational" their direction, Satan keeps them from turning their eyes toward the one and only God.

While I don't believe you need to go looking for Satan under every rock (since he's sitting on top of most of them), you should be aware that not everything is as harmless as it seems. How can you tell what's healthy and what's not? Stay clothed with the "armor of God" (see Ephesians 6:10–18). Have a firm grip on the "sword of the Spirit, which is the word of God." Put on truth and hold high the "shield of faith."

If God is so loving, why does he allow things like rape, abortion, drunk drivers, and murder to happen so often? Can't he do anything to control this stuff?

GENESIS 2:15–17

The Lord God took the man and put him in the Garden of Eden to work it and take care of it. And the Lord God commanded the man, "You are free to eat from any tree in the garden; but you must not eat from the tree of the knowledge of good and evil, for when you eat of it you will surely die."

GENESIS 3:1–6

Now the serpent was more crafty than any of the wild animals the Lord God had made. He said to the woman, "Did God really say, 'You must not eat from any tree in the garden'?"

The woman said to the serpent, "We may eat fruit from the trees in the garden, but God did say, 'You must not eat fruit from the tree that is in the middle of the garden, and you must not touch it, or you will die.' "

"You will not surely die," the serpent said to the woman. "For God knows that when you eat of it your eyes will be opened, and you will be like God, knowing good and evil."

When the woman saw that the fruit of the tree was good for
food and pleasing to the eye, and also desirable for gaining wisdom,
she took some and ate it. She also gave some to her husband, who was
with her, and he ate it.

This is one question that seems to trip up a lot of people: Why do bad things happen? The answer isn't simple, but it is logical.

God's love demanded that he give us free choice. He gave this choice to Adam and Eve in the Garden of Eden—and they used their choice to disobey him. He could have prevented them from doing something this stupid, but he found no satisfaction in creating puppets to bow down to him. Free choice, because of the sinful nature we inherited from Adam and Eve, means people will choose wrong. Wrong choices mean consequences—for everyone. For Adam and Eve, it meant they were banished from the Garden and forced to live their lives separated from God while they lived on earth.

Sadly, Christians aren't immune to the wrong choices of others. Bad things will always happen. But remember, this earth isn't heaven and God never said it would be.

God *does* care about us, but because he loves us, he doesn't try to fix everything bad in the world. That's right. Because he loves us, he chooses to limit his control. You see, in order to make everything in the world happy, he would have to *control* every situation. And if he was pushing the buttons in everyone's life, then people would respond to him out of fear, not love.

If your parents beat you until you told them you loved them, that would give them no satisfaction. Instead, they waited, cared for you until the day—of your own free will— you came to tell them you loved them. God is the same way, even with people who choose to do things that are very bad.

When terrible things happen, it's usually because people have used their God-given freedom of choice to do things against what he wanted. People like you and me sometimes face the consequences for other people's sin.

My parents were both married three times before I was out of high school. God didn't tell them to be selfish and chase others; they did it on their own. Their selfishness had some real negative effects for me. For a while I began taking drugs and completely rejected God's existence. But then I discovered who he really was and how much he loved me.

I also know that if my son reaches up and pulls a pan of scalding hot water on his head that he will be scarred for life. If I'm across the room when he does it, there may be nothing I can do.

I know that if my mom smokes for forty-seven years she may suffer some adverse health effects. Well, she did choose to smoke for all of those years. And for five years she lived like a vegetable before just recently dying from the effects of emphysema. What caused her to suffer all of those years? Her smoking, or God's meanness?

Do you see the difference? God isn't to blame for every bad thing that happens in the world. Frankly, in most situations I have faced or observed, I believe Satan is to blame. He's known as the liar and destroyer. If he can convince people to make poor health or moral choices, he can get them into a lifestyle where they will die young (hopefully, he thinks, without Christ). He's good at keeping people so distracted that the thought of having God at the center of their lives could never be attractive.

We can't see the big picture, but God can. What good came of my parents' divorces? Well, I worked with non-Christian teens for ten years. God literally helped me touch hundreds of lives so they could get through their own tough years. He used my dysfunctional home so that I could relate to those who were facing the same situation. He helped things work out for good, but he certainly didn't cause all those divorces and alcoholic rages I saw as a teenager.

The question really isn't why bad things happen (because they're going to happen). The question is how God can use for his purposes the bad things that do happen.

CHAPTER 8

I have a friend who's always laughing and making fun of me and one of my Christian friends. He doesn't come from a Christian family, but he thinks he's going to heaven. If you looked at his life, there would be no way to tell. I care about him a lot and hope he's going to heaven, but I want to help him be sure.

1 PETER 3:15–17

But in your hearts set apart Christ as Lord. Always be prepared to give an answer to everyone who asks you to give the reason for the hope that you have. But do this with gentleness and respect, keeping a clear conscience, so that those who speak maliciously against your good behavior in Christ may be ashamed of their slander. It is better, if it is God's will, to suffer for doing good than for doing evil.

When your friend said that he thinks he'll go to heaven, he's on pretty shaky ground. A question that many Christians use to find out for sure is, "If you were to die tonight, do you know for certain that you'd go to heaven?" When the time is right to bring up a question like this, ask it.

You said he doesn't come from a Christian family. That

means that if he does become a Christian any number of things might happen.

1. His parents might accept what he's done.
2. They might ignore it.
3. They might ridicule him.
4. They might prevent him from going to church or being involved in things that could help him grow.

I know that if someone doesn't have strong support at home, it's going to be tough for that person to stick with the faith. God has his timing with everyone. Maybe God's allowing him to wait because he knows the people who could spiritually care for him are not yet in place.

The best thing you can do with someone who's putting off this decision is to keep the lines of communication open. The fact that he's laughing at you and your friend tells me he knows there's a difference between you and him. Make sure it's a good difference. Don't let his taunts affect you or get you mad at him. There's a battle going on for his soul. Satan doesn't want him to turn to the Lord. You and your friend need to pray for him every day and, when the time is right, ask him again what's keeping him from turning his life over to the Lord.

Remember this most of all: It's not your or my responsibility to save this guy; it's God's. It's our responsibility to be available for God to use us. That may mean planting seeds in his life or, perhaps at a later date, reaping the harvest of his soul for Christ. Be patient and persevering, but most of all, be available to him—and others—especially during these days you have in school.

I'm having trouble letting other people know I'm a Christian. I'm afraid they'll laugh at me or ask a question I can't answer.

EXODUS 4:1

Moses answered, "What if they do not believe me or listen to me and say, 'The Lord did not appear to you'?"

The Bible is filled with examples of people who faced the choice of either being courageous or letting their fears tell them how to act. Learning about the courage of people in the Bible is one good reason to read it every day. The examples we find in the pages of that book can give us the strength to step out in faith and do things that may *at first* seem very frightening.

In Exodus 3, God had just finished speaking with Moses through a burning bush. Although this was an incredible miracle, Exodus 4 relates how Moses was afraid people wouldn't believe that God had actually spoken to him. He had to choose between giving in to his fears or facing them head-on. Eventually, Moses chose to draw courage from God, and he completed the task God had given him.

Whether it's riding a bike for the first time, going down a steep hill on a skateboard, or driving a car, there's always an element of the unknown that can only be overcome by doing what you think is frightening. Repeating an action until you can do it well enough to enjoy it develops character and skill. This is true with everything from snow skiing to volleyball—and it's true in telling your best friends on earth about your Friend in heaven.

God doesn't expect you to know all the answers, either. When the apostle Peter was confronted by the hostile religious leaders of the day who told him to stop talking about Jesus, he answered, "For we cannot help speaking about what we have seen and heard" (Acts 4:20). He had learned the joy of sharing his faith in Christ so much that he couldn't help but share what he knew.

You have the privilege and the responsibility of sharing what you've learned and what God has done in your life. If you don't know an answer to a question, you can always say, "That's a good question. Can I find out the answer and get back with you in a couple of days?"

The key to Moses's decision to obey God's command to be his spokesman for the Israelites was his remembering when God first spoke to him. The burning bush experience and God's continuing miracles gave Moses the courage to face incredible obstacles. Stuff like Pharaoh's army, the Red Sea, forty years in the wilderness—none of these obstacles kept Moses from following through.

10

If I obey God like I read I'm supposed to, will I get anything more than a clear conscience?

JOHN 14:23

Jesus replied, "If anyone loves me he will obey my teaching. My Father will love him, and we will come to him and make our home with him."

Although a clear conscience doesn't seem like much these days, some psychologists say that fifty percent of the people in mental hospitals could go home if they knew they were forgiven. There are real advantages in keeping a clear conscience before God.

Obedience to God will always have a reward, but it is also a command (John 14:15). This means it's our choice to either obey or disobey. The story of Abraham and Isaac is a great example of the rewards of obedience.

To most fathers, the command to sacrifice a son would clearly be one to disobey. Yet Abraham loved God so much that he trusted him, even with the future of his only son.

Abraham needed to be tested by God to see if he was worthy of being the father of faith for the entire world. Abraham proved himself worthy by his obedience. As a result, Isaac was spared and Abraham's faith became the example for everyone seeking to know how to please God (see Hebrews 11:1–2, 17–19).

God rewards his children for their obedience. "And without faith it is impossible to please God, because anyone who comes to him must believe that he exists and that he rewards those who earnestly seek him" (Hebrews 11:6).

Sometimes the rewards are immediate; other times God chooses to delay them. It's usually during the times when God chooses to delay our rewards that we begin to wonder if obedience to God is really worth it. God's command to stay sexually pure until marriage doesn't necessarily come with any immediate rewards. And if you have idiots for friends, they may even put you down for not having lost your virginity yet. But if you give God time to bring the right person into your life, and stay pure while you're waiting, God will typically give you a spouse beyond your wildest dreams. He does stuff like that.

When God delays his rewards, he is waiting to see if we are obeying him out of love or if we are obeying him for what we'll receive. God can't be manipulated into giving us things we aren't ready to handle. Sometimes we need to be tested first in smaller areas to show that we can handle larger rewards or responsibilities without becoming prideful.

Obey God, and leave the rewards to him. In the long run, he won't let you down. Guaranteed.

CHAPTER 11

I became a Christian at a big youth rally last fall. Afterward, I felt great for a few days. I knew that having a relationship with God was something I wanted. But soon my good feelings went away. Did I lose him? Why didn't the good feelings stay around?

1 JOHN 5:10–21

Anyone who believes in the Son of God has this testimony in his heart. Anyone who does not believe God has made him out to be a liar, because he has not believed the testimony God has given about his Son. And this is the testimony: God has given us eternal life, and this life is in his Son. He who has the Son has life; he who does not have the Son of God does not have life.

Picture yourself meeting your favorite TV or music superstar face-to-face. It would be an experience that you'd likely never forget. Yet over time you'd eventually forget the intensity of the emotion you once felt. Would it mean that you didn't actually meet this person? No, but it does illustrate that our feelings often come and go based on what's happened to us recently.

Asking Jesus Christ into your life is far better than meeting another human, famous or not. What you've begun is a lifelong relationship with the God who created everything. He actually wants to live in you so that you'll live forever *and* so others can see that he really loves them, too.

In John 14:23 Jesus says, "I will only reveal myself to those who love me and obey me. The Father will love them too, and we will come to them and live with them" (TLB). The phrase *live with them* actually means "build a mansion" in them. God wants to come into your life and make something extraordinary out of it. He has begun a process of molding your character to become more like that of Jesus Christ. Within this lifelong process will be some good feelings, but more often we will not have continual, intense excitement.

Getting to know someone as loving and forgiving as Jesus Christ is similar to other relationships you enjoy. There is the initial experience of meeting a person, followed by months and years of growing to appreciate his or her friendship and influence. Anything worthwhile takes time.

Once you've genuinely chosen to follow Jesus Christ, you can never lose him. He will always be there in your life to guide and love you in the midst of all that our world may throw your way. This should outweigh your tendency to base your relationship with God on your up-and-down feelings.

CHAPTER
12

If Christ controls my life, where does my freedom of choice fit in?

JOSHUA 24:14–15

Now fear the Lord and serve him with all faithfulness.
Throw away the gods your forefathers worshiped beyond the River
and in Egypt, and serve the Lord. But if serving the Lord seems
undesirable to you, then choose for yourselves this day whom you will
serve, whether the gods your forefathers served beyond the River, or
the gods of the Amorites, in whose land you are living. But as for me
and my household, we will serve the Lord.

One way that God demonstrated his love to us was by giving us the freedom of choice. Just as wise parents don't discipline their child until they say, "I love you," God doesn't resort to strong-arm tactics, either. He actively shows his love to each soul and then allows them the choice as to whether to respond to it.

Someone once said, "There is a door to your heart that can only be opened from the inside." You made the choice to open the door of your heart to Jesus Christ when you received him as Savior and Lord. Although his Spirit was at work prompting you to respond to his love, the choice was yours. But do your choices about God stop there?

Imagine your life as a house. Jesus Christ knocked on the front door, and you decided to let him in (see Revelation 3:20). Where do you invite him next? Some Christians live their whole lives with Christ still standing in the entryway. Obviously this isn't a very good way to treat an invited guest! But it happens because people want to use their freedom of choice to stay in control of their own lives. They want heaven, but not much else.

During your entire life as a Christian, you'll use your God-given freedom of choice to invite him into the rest of your house (your life) or to leave him at the front door.

Although your life is much more complicated than a house, let's take the illustration one step further. In your house you probably have rooms that need repair. The living room, for example, could represent your relationships at home. How does the room look? When problems occur in this room, the solution is to ask the master carpenter, Jesus, for some renovation. Through his Word, other people, and the prodding of the Holy Spirit, God gently tells us how to make things right.

This passage in Joshua tells of God's challenge to the nation of Israel: "Then you must destroy all the idols you now own, and you must obey the Lord God of Israel" (Joshua 24:23, TLB). The Israelites were faced with a choice of whom they were going to serve. On that day, they chose to serve the living God instead of idols made by human hands.

Every day you'll be faced with the choice of serving God . . . or something else: money, popularity, pleasure. God loves you too much to take that choice away from you, even if it means you'll occasionally make the wrong choice.

He has given to you the privilege of having him come into every area of your life—your language, what you put in front of your eyes, what you listen to. Trust him to know what he's doing: say yes to the choices you know God wants you to make.

Which is more important to do, *live* like a Christian or *tell* others about my faith in Christ?

2 KINGS 7:3-9

*Now there were four men with leprosy at the entrance of the
city gate. They said to each other, "Why stay here until we die? If we
say, 'We'll go into the city'—the famine is there, and we will die.
And if we stay here, we will die. So let's go over to the camp of the
Arameans and surrender. If they spare us, we live; if they kill us,
then we die."*

*At dusk they got up and went to the camp of the Arameans.
When they reached the edge of the camp, not a man was there, for the
Lord had caused the Arameans to hear the sound of chariots and
horses and a great army, so that they said to one another, "Look, the
king of Israel has hired the Hittite and Egyptian kings to attack us!"
So they got up and fled in the dusk and abandoned their tents and
their horses and donkeys. They left the camp as it was and ran for
their lives.*

*The men who had leprosy reached the edge of the camp and
entered one of the tents. They ate and drank, and carried away silver,
gold and clothes, and went off and hid them. They returned and
entered another tent and took some things from it and hid them also.*

*Then they said to each other, "We're not doing right. This is
a day of good news and we are keeping it to ourselves. If we wait until*

daylight, punishment will overtake us. Let's go at once and report this to the royal palace."

Try to remember the best Christmas present you ever received. For me it was a red bike. I quickly took it for a spin over to my friend's house to show him how cool it was. At five-thirty in the morning his family was opening their presents next to their front room window. While everyone watched, I circled their cul-de-sac . . . and promptly fell flat on my face. (So much for showing off.) What did you typically do after your family was through opening presents? More than likely, you called your best friends to tell them about what you got. It was so cool, you couldn't *not* tell them.

Forgiveness from sin is absolutely the greatest gift you will ever receive! It's impossible to keep quiet about it if you truly recognize how important this free gift really is. Which, unfortunately, is sometimes tough for teenagers.

Compare the four men with leprosy who discovered the empty camp to a group of five-year-olds waking up Christmas morning with more presents than they could ever open! The joy and amazement the lepers experienced was beyond their wildest dreams. God had given them something that was simply too wonderful to keep to themselves.

Unfortunately, some people—even adults—take for granted the gift of salvation through Jesus Christ. These are often the people who say little about their faith. They're glad they won't have to go to hell, but not glad enough to help keep someone else from going there.

For other Christians, having Christ as Savior is the most exciting present they have ever been given! Of course, having a present does not automatically mean that others will know about it. We must tell them.

Our sin is like leprosy. We can't always tell its effects, but left unchecked, the disease gets progressively worse. Having our sins cleansed when we receive the gift of forgiveness through Christ should bring the same joy a leper would have when suddenly cleansed.

Salvation should be received *and* given away. It's like breathing and a heartbeat. You have to have both to live. And Christians—if they're really going to live—must receive God's gift and give it away. Our response in thankfulness to God, we hope, should not cause us to just hold the gift but to give it to all who will take it.

CHAPTER 14

Now that I'm a Christian, how should I act around my friends and family who aren't?

MARK 5:18–20

As Jesus was getting into the boat, the man who had been demon-possessed begged to go with him. Jesus did not let him, but said, "Go home to your family and tell them how much the Lord has done for you, and how he has had mercy on you." So the man went away and began to tell in the Decapolis how much Jesus had done for him. And all the people were amazed.

The most important thing you have going for you in both sets of relationships is that you already have a "relational bridge" in place. They knew what your life was like before you met Christ. Now they will have the chance to see you afterward.

Jesus recognized that this was the case with the man he had just cleansed from demon possession. He sent him back to his home to be an example to others instead of asking him to leave those who knew him best.

Another passage calls us Christ's ambassadors to our world (see 2 Corinthians 5:17–20). This means we are his hand-picked representatives. If people want to know what God is like, all they have to do is look at us.

God doesn't expect you to be perfect, but he does expect that your faith will grow (Romans 10:17) and that you will try to live more like Jesus Christ would each day (Romans 12:1–2).

It's progress—not perfection—that people around you will be able to relate to. Progress may be slow at first, but eventually, if you're giving areas of your life to Christ's control, people will begin to notice the change. Hopefully, they'll also start to ask questions about your new faith.

Although you may *feel* inadequate answering some of their questions, your responsibility is only to share what God has done for you and what you have learned, not to be the Bible-answer genius. Remember, it's God's job to save people, not yours. He's at work in the hearts of all humans, drawing them to himself. Some respond, many don't.

Please know that it's just as important (and biblical) to share and live your faith as a new Christian as it is to be more mature in the faith or a Bible scholar. God is not limited by our lack of knowledge.

Like the demon-possessed man whose life Jesus changed, you may have faced many unique hardships. As a new Christian, your changed life will have a greater impact on your friends, those with whom relational bridges have already been built, than will the words of a stranger, however eloquently he may speak.

15

When I read about creation and miracles in the Bible, I get confused. How do science and the Bible relate?

GENESIS 2:4–7

This is the account of the heavens and the earth when they were created.

When the Lord God made the earth and heavens—and no shrub of the field had yet appeared on the earth and no plant of the field had yet sprung up, for the Lord God had not sent rain on the earth and there was no man to work the ground, but streams came up from the earth and watered the whole surface of the ground—the Lord God formed the man from the dust of the ground and breathed into his nostrils the breath of life, and man became a living being.

The Bible-versus-science debate has raged for centuries. Conflict will always arise when we try to look for spiritual answers from science or scientific answers from the Bible.

A former Vietnam POW told of the time he was allowed to send a cassette tape home to his family. Realizing that it might be the last communication he would ever have with those he loved, he made extensive notes on what he would cover before he began to make the tape. His goal was to communicate the most important things his family should know. To his wife, he talked of insurance, mortgages, child rearing, and relatives. To the kids, he personalized each message so that he touched on unique situations they would face in the next few years as they grew up without him. To all of them he made sure he told how much he loved them.

This is exactly the purpose behind the Bible. God put sixty-six books together to let his creation know the most important things about life, about what to do in certain situations, and especially about the extent of his love for them.

For some reason he chose to leave out dinosaurs, fusion, and gravity (among other significant discoveries). Instead, he included stories of real people with real struggles who faced hardship and trials, many of whom conquered fears and circumstances because they realized that if God was for them, who could be against them! Still other stories are included of those who rejected God and then experienced the tragic consequences.

Most of these biblical examples tell us much more about living, surviving, and prospering in a complicated society than science could ever hope to promise.

Your mind matters to God—he wants you to think. Never be afraid to ask tough questions about the Bible or the Christian faith. But also consider the appropriateness of each question: Is this the kind of question the Bible *should* answer? And do the same with science, asking the right questions.

Creation and the resurrection of Jesus Christ are two of the most important tenets of the Christian faith. Although they can't be duplicated in a laboratory, they also can't be proven false by science.

If God can create life from nothing, as well as raise a man from the dead, he can guide us through this life *and* the next. We can trust him.

CHAPTER 16

The Old Testament is long and sometimes boring.

Why did God put it in the Bible?

DEUTERONOMY 1:8

See, I have given you this land. Go in and take possession of the land that the Lord swore he would give to your fathers—to Abraham, Isaac and Jacob—and to their descendants after them.

What if you asked your grandfather to tell you his whole life story? You'd probably receive an all-day talk, full of wonderful memories that would be fun for your grandfather, but you'd eventually get bored because you'd hear too many facts that wouldn't relate to your life.

But if you just asked him to relate the top ten experiences that shaped his personality and helped him make it through life, it would not only take a lot less time, it would likely be fascinating. You'd learn a lot about why your grandpa is the way he is.

Though it may sometimes seem like it, the Old Testament isn't a detailed day-by-day account of history. Instead, it's the story of God working through the Jewish people to bring the world the Messiah. Their history points directly to Jesus Christ. Through this story, we see God's plan of sending his Son, Jesus, to die on the cross to pay the penalty for our sin.

Living hundreds of years after all these facts limits our appreciation that for three thousand years, the Old Testament has guided people from every walk of life. It was not just written for people in our day, but also for people who needed to hear from God in A.D. 320 Rome or A.D. 1540 Germany.

What this means is that not every story will affect you the way it has others through the years. But as you read through the Old Testament, you'll be surprised at how many stories relate to you today.

God's command to Moses and the Israelites to go into the Promised Land and possess it is the fulfillment of a promise to Abraham that God made long before Moses was even born. It shows that God has a plan for history—and that he keeps his promises. It is absolutely essential for you as a Christian to realize that your heavenly Father keeps his promises! This allows us to give him control of our lives because for centuries he has proven himself trustworthy. (See Hebrews 11 for a brief recap of God's faithfulness.)

The Old Testament also tells us about the real-life struggles people experienced when faced with the choice between trusting God and doing things their own way. Instead of giving us all of history to read, God condensed his story into one book. He has even pointed out the most important lessons we need to pay attention to in order to live life to the fullest as his children.

CHAPTER 17

I like the people in my church, but sometimes the worship service seems boring and confusing. Are all of the songs, readings, and rituals necessary?

2 CHRONICLES 20:20–22

Early in the morning they left for the Desert of Tekoa. As they set out, Jehoshaphat stood and said, "Listen to me, Judah and people of Jerusalem! Have faith in the Lord your God and you will be upheld; have faith in his prophets and you will be successful." After consulting the people, Jehoshaphat appointed men to sing to the Lord and to praise him for the splendor of his holiness as they went out at the head of the army, saying: "Give thanks to the Lord, for his love endures forever."

As they began to sing and praise, the Lord set ambushes against the men of Ammon and Moab and Mount Seir who were invading Judah, and they were defeated.

A family decided to get a new refrigerator, so they bought one that was the top of the line and filled it with groceries. It was Friday, and they had a trip out of town planned for the weekend, so they left. When they returned on Sunday, they opened the refrigerator door and were overwhelmed by a terrible odor. All of the food had spoiled!

There had been no power failure, and the refrigerator wasn't broken. Instead, they had forgotten to plug it in! Their brand-new appliance, stuffed with food, was useless (and smelly) without being plugged into the power.

We need to be plugged in, too, and worship is one way to do this. In worship we recognize God as the one who is in control and who has the power to change our circumstances and lives.

Jehoshaphat discovered this fact very graphically as he sent the worshipers out with his army. As the worshipers were singing, God miraculously provided a victory.

Worship takes many forms. Most of the songs and readings come right from Scripture. If you concentrate on the meaning behind what is being sung or read, you'll see that the words communicate very important facts about God.

When we sing a song many times, we'll memorize it more easily. You can probably sing every word of your favorite popular songs. Music helps us remember, even if it isn't the style we like best.

Another purpose of worship is to encourage us to grow in our faith. With all of the negative influences around us, we need to be filled with courage to go out to face the world. This courage can help us live the Christian life when it seems that there's a war going on around us.

Worship is also the time for us to praise God for who he is and to thank him for all he's done. And worshiping together in church with our brothers and sisters in Christ is like a family reunion.

Ephesians 5:19 was written during a time when Christians were put in prison for their faith. It says, "Talk with each other much about the Lord, quoting psalms and hymns and singing sacred songs, making music in your hearts to the Lord" (TLB). By doing what this verse talks about they were able to encourage one another as they reminded themselves of the faithfulness, goodness, and strength of God.

CHAPTER 18

I grew up in church, but I'm starting to feel like
I don't fit in anymore. Most of my friends don't
go to church. What's wrong with my faith?

ROMANS 8:38–39

*For I am convinced that neither death nor life, neither angels
nor demons, neither the present nor the future, nor any powers,
neither height nor depth, nor anything else in all creation,
will be able to separate us from the love of God that is in
Christ Jesus our Lord.*

The first place to check when the "feelings" taper off is
your own heart. If you're feeling guilty because you've disobeyed God, admit your sin, ask God for forgiveness, and
reopen communication with him. Perhaps you're not feeling
too good because there's a broken human relationship that
needs mending. If so, make it right.

To be honest, the Christian life isn't about feelings. Most
of the time our feeling meter will be set on "normal." You
see, Christians experience the whole range of emotions as
well as anyone else. They're happy, sad, fearful, angry, lonely,
excited, apprehensive, and so on. Whatever the reason for
these feelings, Christians feel them all at one time or another. That's what it means to be human and to live in an
imperfect world.

Fortunately, your relationship with God doesn't depend
on how you feel. It's based on *facts*, not feelings. It's a fact

that Jesus died for you and that he rose from the dead. It's a fact that you gave your life by faith to him. It's a fact that you are a new creation, bearing the mark of ownership of the Holy Spirit (see 2 Corinthians 5:17), and it is yours regardless of how you now feel.

Some people think that Christians should always be happy and confident, but that doesn't match what God says in his Word. We are told to "share the sorrow" of those who are sad (Romans 12:15). And Jesus wept because of the unbelief and grief he saw in people around him (John 11:35). Later, Jesus promised his disciples that on earth they would have many trials and sorrows (John 16:33).

The Christians in Rome underwent severe persecution—many were tortured and killed because they believed in Christ. Surely they were torn with grief and pain. Yet Paul wrote to them (and to us) that nothing can ever separate us from God's love (Romans 8:39).

Christians experience all sorts of circumstances, struggles, and emotions. But the fantastic news is that no matter where we are, what we're facing, or what we're feeling, God is with us, and we can never lose his love.

What does God really expect from me? I hear different things from so many people that I'm overwhelmed. I feel like I have to give up a lot in order to make God happy.

GENESIS 4:2-7

Now Abel kept flocks, and Cain worked the soil. In the course of time Cain brought some of the fruits of the soil as an offering to the Lord. But Abel brought fat portions from some of the firstborn of his flock. The Lord looked with favor on Abel and his offering, but on Cain and his offering he did not look with favor. So Cain was very angry, and his face was downcast.

Then the Lord said to Cain, "Why are you angry? Why is your face downcast? If you do what is right, will you not be accepted? But if you do not do what is right, sin is crouching at your door; it desires to have you, but you must master it."

One essential quality of God is that he's very personal with *each* Christian. And although he chooses not to treat everyone alike, he *does* have expectations of his kids.

Some Christians may tell you about God's expectations based on where they are in their walk with him. If too many people are giving you advice, it could seem as though God expects way too much. This doesn't mean that you should quit listening to sincere Christians who want to help. It does mean, however, that if you're feeling overwhelmed, you're probably listening too much to others and not enough to God.

So what do you do? How do you please God?

The example from this story of Cain and Abel gives a significant piece to the puzzle. Each of these men brought something to God, but only Abel's sacrifice pleased him. One reason was that Cain's heart wasn't really in it. He tried to please God out of obligation instead of love.

The first key to pleasing God is found in our heart or our motivation. Do we really want to make God happy, or are we going through the motions because someone told us we should?

The second key to pleasing God is obedience. "The one who obeys me is the one who loves me; and because he loves me, my Father will love him; and I will too, and I will reveal myself to him" (John 14:21, TLB).

Good parents want their children to obey them in the essentials of how to live, how to avoid situations that will lead to pain or scars, and how to treat other people.

God is no different. But he's the perfect Father. Obedience to God is loving him enough to listen to what he says, then following through on what we know he is telling us.

This is why reading the Bible every day is so important. We cannot obey what we don't know. All that God wants us to know is written very plainly in his Word. Through the Holy Spirit, God speaks to us as we come to him with willing hearts. He gently shows us areas in our lives that we need to examine and change according to *his* timetable, not someone else's.

A friend says that my new faith in Christ is too narrow because Christians believe Christ is the only way to God. Why can't God accept different ideas by other religions?

JUDGES 17:6

In those days Israel had no king; everyone did as he saw fit.

Suppose your history teacher told you that Columbus discovered America in 1492. Just then, four other people raised their hands and said, "I think he discovered America in 1454 (or 1678 or 1543 or 1733). What makes you the authority on history anyway? We're going to believe what we think is right."

Do these kids have the freedom to believe what they think is right? Of course they do.

A wise teacher would likely respond, "You may believe any date you choose, but there is only one right answer and I have told you what it is. If you put a different answer on the test at the end of the term, it will be marked wrong."

God has given people the freedom to choose what they want to believe about who he is and what his plan is for human beings. But when the test scores are graded at the end of the age, there will be only one right answer.

This verse from Judges comes from a period in Jewish history when they had no leader. "Everyone did whatever he wanted to—whatever seemed right in his own eyes" (TLB).

What this means is that not only did people choose to disobey God as their leader, but their actions were evil, as well. Throughout history people have behaved according to what they believed about God.

If people believe that God doesn't exist or that God doesn't care how we live and treat each other, they will likely act accordingly. Usually, this means that they treat themselves or others like there will be no final exam when they pass on to the next life!

Jesus said, "I am the way and the truth and the life. No one comes to the Father except through me" (John 14:6). This means that God grades on a pass/fail basis depending on what we have done with his Son, Jesus.

God has given people the freedom to believe any "religion" they want. But the final authority is not their own beliefs. There is only one right answer. God's standard is faith in Jesus Christ, his death on the cross, and his resurrection so that our sin would not eternally separate us from God.

CHAPTER 21

Does God get tired of hearing about our troubles? I get frustrated sometimes when I see myself in the same problems over and over again.

PSALM 88:1-9

O Lord, the God who saves me, day and night I cry out
before you. May my prayer come before you; turn your ear to my cry.
For my soul is full of trouble and my life draws near the grave. I am
counted among those who go down to the pit; I am like a man without
strength. I am set apart with the dead, like the slain who lie in the
grave, whom you remember no more, who are cut off from your care.
You have put me in the lowest pit, in the darkest depths. Your wrath
lies heavily upon me; you have overwhelmed me with all your waves.

You have taken from me my closest friends and have made me
repulsive to them. I am confined and cannot escape; my eyes are dim
with grief. I call to you, O Lord, every day; I spread out my
hands to you.

Do you know someone who likes to complain a lot? Perhaps you have a little brother, a friend, or just someone you know at school who is always griping. They probably aren't very much fun to be around.

Complaining means two things. First, we aren't happy with what's going on around us. We think that by telling others we want something to change, it will happen. Second, it means we want attention. Complaining focuses the spotlight on us for a brief moment. In that moment, people are giving us the attention we think we need. Sometimes, that's all we really wanted in the first place!

If you've ever read through the Psalms, you've seen that David seems to complain . . . a lot! He's always in some sort of trouble and he wants God to get him out of it. Sound familiar?

The key issue behind our complaining is the motivation. When surrounded by enemies, David cried to God for protection. He had nowhere else to turn. Although this may seem like complaining, it actually is a very real way to pray. God never gets tired of hearing us *and* coming to our rescue if we need his help.

Sometimes when we complain or ask God for help it's because we've made wrong choices that have gotten us into trouble. We didn't study for a test, it's fifty percent of our grade, and now we want God to supernaturally give us the knowledge we would have had if we spent a few less hours in front of the TV. Our natural response is to ask God to get us out of it. Though God always listens and lends a sympathetic ear, he knows the solution is not his coming to the rescue.

Instead, we must ask for forgiveness for saying something we shouldn't have or doing something we knew might come back to haunt us (like laziness, gossip, anger, and resentment). In his own gentle way, God can show us that some troubles are best solved by being humble and admitting we were wrong.

If trouble comes from people or situations that are beyond our control, God is not only quick to hear but also quick to answer. Either he will provide the internal resources necessary to handle the problem: "You will experience God's peace, which is far more wonderful than the human mind can understand" (Philippians 4:7, TLB). Or he will provide the way of escape: "No temptation has seized you except what is common to man. And God is faithful; he will not let you be tempted beyond what you can bear. But when you are tempted, he will also provide a way out so that you can stand up under it" (1 Corinthians 10:13).

CHAPTER 22

I heard something about a sin that God cannot forgive. What is it?

PSALM 51:1–12

Have mercy on me, O God, according to your unfailing love; according to your great compassion blot out my transgressions. Wash away all my iniquity and cleanse me from my sin. For I know my transgressions, and my sin is always before me. Against you, you only, have I sinned and done what is evil in your sight, so that you are proved right when you speak and justified when you judge.

Surely I was sinful from birth, sinful from the time my mother conceived me. Surely you desire truth in the inner parts; you teach me wisdom in the inmost place. Cleanse me with hyssop, and I will be clean; wash me, and I will be whiter than snow. Let me hear joy and gladness; let the bones you have crushed rejoice.

Hide your face from my sins and blot out all my iniquity. Create in me a pure heart, O God, and renew a steadfast spirit within me. Do not cast me from your presence or take your Holy Spirit from me. Restore to me the joy of your salvation and grant me a willing spirit, to sustain me.

What you're referring to is sinning against the Holy Spirit. "Even blasphemy against me or any other sin, can be forgiven—all except one: speaking against the Holy Spirit shall never be forgiven, either in this world or in the world to come" (Matthew 12:31–32, TLB).

As you read in this psalm, everyone is born a sinner (verse 5). Left to ourselves, we'd surely die because our sinful nature is the part in us that God cannot hang around with. He's just too holy and pure to be associated with the darkness of our sin.

The good news is God didn't leave us to ourselves. He took the sins of each person who ever lived and placed them on his sinless Son, Jesus. By doing this, he killed sin forever. Everyone who receives his Son into their lives and accepts his gift of forgiveness is forgiven—period (see John 1:12).

The only sin that cannot be forgiven is when someone, for their entire lifetime, refuses to listen to the Holy Spirit's "voice" when he reveals to them the way of escape from the penalty of their sin. It is the continual attitude of rebellion and deliberate rejection of the Holy Spirit that is unforgivable.

The incident that caused King David to pray the prayer in Psalm 51 is found in 2 Samuel 12:1–23. David not only committed adultery, but he had the woman's husband murdered so he could marry her! Pretty raunchy behavior for a king.

When confronted with his sin a year after those events, David repented. He asked God to forgive and renew their relationship; to make it clean like it had been in the past. Though David's sins were great, it's a perfect example of how God is always willing to forgive those who are strong enough to admit their mistakes and who genuinely try not to do them again.

It has been said, "The only sin God cannot forgive is the one we have not confessed."

By daily coming to God in humility, trust, and dependence, we show him that we mean business in keeping our relationship with him clean and growing.

David's prayer is the perfect example of a humble heart seeking after the only thing in life that really matters—a close relationship with God.

CHAPTER 23

A friend of mine quit coming to church because he said that God had stopped answering his prayers. How do I respond to him?

2 TIMOTHY 4:9–10

Do your best to come to me quickly, for Demas, because he loved this world, has deserted me and has gone to Thessalonica. Crescens has gone to Galatia, and Titus to Dalmatia.

Like Demas, who deserted Paul, many Christians have a what-have-you-done-for-me-lately type of faith in God. They're willing to trust him in the good times, but when trouble hits, they figure that since God seems to have checked out on them, they'll just check out on God.

Of course, we often do this with people. When Mom or Dad fails to meet our expectations in some way, we're tempted to think they no longer care.

A person with a good memory and a sensitive heart, however, soon realizes that Mom and Dad have sacrificed a lot over the years for the sake of their kids. Just because they put the hammer down a couple of times on what could have been fun doesn't mean they no longer care or are insensitive to our needs. It means that in their judgment, a certain activity or privilege would not be in our best interest over the long haul.

Because we live in a society where we can often get what we want when we want it, we may drift toward a belief in a

God whose only purpose is to meet our needs. Then when something doesn't work out—when we think God hasn't come through for us—we turn away from him.

God is in the business of molding our character to look like his Son, Jesus. One way he does this is by allowing us to go through tough times. When Paul wrote the above letter, the church was going through intense persecution. Demas got tired of it and left. He wanted the comforts of the present world more than he wanted to stick it out until the end.

Encourage your friend to change the what-have-you-done-for-me-lately-God attitude. Help him realize that God wants to build his character. God's goal isn't to make us feel good all the time, but to bring others to the realization that our God can be their God, as well.

My parents are quietly putting up with my new faith. Mom thinks it's "nice," and Dad won't talk to me about it. How do I make them see Jesus is a real person?

MATTHEW 10:34–39

*"Do not suppose that I have come to bring peace to the earth.
I did not come to bring peace, but a sword. For I have come to turn 'a
man against his father, a daughter against her mother, a daughter-in-
law against her mother-in-law—a man's enemies will be the members
of his own household.'*

*"Anyone who loves his father or mother more than me is not
worthy of me; anyone who loves his son or daughter more than me is
not worthy of me; and anyone who does not take his cross and follow
me is not worthy of me. Whoever finds his life will lose it, and
whoever loses his life for my sake will find it."*

There are many difficult sayings of Jesus in the New Testament. This is one of the toughest. What does he mean when he says, "A man's enemies will be the members of his own household"?

If you have faced pressure from friends at school because of your new faith, you realize that commitment to Christ causes people to make decisions about *you*. Some will stay with you and support your decision because they are your true friends. Others will leave because they don't understand. Some will quit calling you because your values no longer encourage their lifestyle.

We may also find opposition at home. Jesus isn't telling us to be disobedient to our parents or to try to cause problems at home. He's just stating a fact that a person with different goals, values, purposes, perhaps even morals, may cause division. More than a fact, it's a promise! Rarely will the only Christian in a household go unchallenged.

Though it is uncommon for parents to be openly hostile toward someone in their home, it does happen. Put-downs or verbal neglect can really hurt, especially if they come from someone you love. The best course of action is to not try to *make* your parents see anything. Instead, just live your life in obedience to them as the Bible commands.

"Children, obey your parents; this is the right thing to do because God has placed them in authority over you. Honor your father and mother. This is the first of God's Ten Commandments that ends with a promise. And this is the promise: that if you honor your father and mother, yours will be a long life, full of blessing" (Ephesians 6:1–3, TLB).

It's not your role to make them change. That is the job of the Holy Spirit (see John 16:8). You are to be God's representative in your home, hopefully to bring your family to faith in Christ.

Don't neglect your family because they don't yet accept your faith. But don't neglect the higher mission of keeping God as your number one priority, either.

The test will come if they tell you that you cannot go to church. You must obey and seek after needed fellowship with God and others by different means.

Find some Christian friends who will pray *for you* and pray *with you* about your situation. Go to them when you need encouragement and advice on how to respond as each difficult situation arises.

I've grown up in a Christian family and believed in God all my life. But recently I realized I've been living off of the faith of my parents. How do I have a faith that's mine?

1 CHRONICLES 28:9

And you, my son Solomon, acknowledge the God of your father, and serve him with whole-hearted devotion and with a willing mind, for the Lord searches every heart and understands every motive behind the thoughts. If you seek him, he will be found by you; but if you forsake him, he will reject you forever.

This may be the most significant realization of your life. Some young people never understand that God wants us to know him personally. Living off of someone else's faith is like borrowing something from friends. Whether you borrow their bike, clothes, skateboard, Walkman and tapes, anything, it isn't yours and must eventually be returned.

Solomon was challenged to get to know the God of his fathers. In other words, he shouldn't settle for hearing how someone else trusted God. He should get to know God for himself.

During these teenage years, your faith will constantly be tested on what you believe about God. Friends who don't believe in Christ may see nothing wrong with doing things that would cause your conscience to start screaming in your ear. During those moments, you'll have to make a choice—do I go along with my friends or do I stand on what I believe?

If *your* faith is strong—instead of being borrowed from your parents or your youth—no amount of pressure from friends will be able to blow you away (see Matthew 7:21–29).

A good example is what you believe about yourself. Your friends who aren't Christians usually rely on looks, money, or athletic ability in order to feel worthwhile. If someone is homely, poor, and uncoordinated, the kids at school can be very cruel in how they treat them.

Are any kids worthless because they don't look like a model, don't have money to spend, or can't throw a baseball? Definitely not! But it could be a natural conclusion they could draw about themselves if they were treated that way. Unless, of course, they knew that the God who created everything actually chose to become one of us, die on a cross to take away our sin, and invite us to live with him forever in heaven as his kids.

Does God think we are valuable? The answer is obvious. But without the foundation of knowing Christ personally, we may never realize God's great love for us. Consider taking these steps to help you develop your own faith.

First, make sure you have asked Jesus Christ to forgive your sin and come into your life, this time doing it for you, not to please someone else.

Second, begin to ask questions about the Bible. God wants you to *understand* it as well as *believe* and *obey* it. God is not afraid of honest questions asked with good motives.

Third, look and pray for other Christians who are excited about developing their faith in God—people who don't want to settle for second best. Being around growing Christians is contagious. What you learn from them will convince you that being a Christian is worth the work and is one hundred percent right—for *you*!

CHAPTER 26

It always seems like I'm giving in to my friends. Lots of times I end up doing stuff I know a Christian shouldn't do. How do I stand up to the pressure?

PROVERBS 1:10

My son, if sinners entice you, do not give in to them.

If each young person had a dollar for every time friends said to "come along," most could pay for college!

Being included feels great. And everyone needs friends to hang around with. But as you know, friends don't always have our best welfare at heart. In fact, sometimes they only want us to join them so they can feel better about doing whatever it is they want to do.

Whether it's pressure to do good things like helping a widow with her yard work, doing homework, or just having a burger, or more questionable things like going to parties where you know alcohol or drugs will be, vandalism, or watching movies your folks don't normally let you watch— pressure to follow others can be pretty intense.

But when kids invite you to go with them to a questionable (or bad) situation and you give in, you haven't just succumbed to peer pressure, you have deliberately lied. We conceal our real character in a split-second decision. All with the *hope* of being liked by a group or a person we *think* has more going for them than our current group.

Our hope, of course, is to have more and "better" friends. Believe it or not, this often works. If it didn't, people wouldn't constantly give in to peer pressure.

We are all tempted to bend our beliefs in order for someone to like us. During the teenage years, the pressure can be intense. It's the hungry urge to do what others are doing to fit in.

Though falling into peer pressure is actually lying, God understands there's a strong urge within us to be included by the group. What does he think about this pressure?

He knows it's strong and he doesn't want to sit idly by, hoping you'll have the strength to put up a fight. He wants to provide the inner muscle it takes to combat the outer pressure you feel.

Remember when your mom or dad taught you to do something like bake cookies or start a lawn mower? They didn't just *tell* you to do it, they *showed* you how.

God wants to show you how to withstand the outer pressure by giving you the internal resources necessary. The actions and words of Jesus and other writers in the Bible can give you the tools to do what's right.

Verses like, "Don't copy the behavior and customs of this world, but be a new and different person with a fresh newness in all you do and think" (Romans 12:2, TLB), help keep us from straying off the path. And sometimes we just have to realize that the consequences aren't worth the risk.

CHAPTER 27

After I became a Christian I was told to start reading the Bible. I had one my grandma gave me, but it's hard to understand and it's bigger than any book I have ever even attempted to read. Where do I start?

JOHN 20:30–31

Jesus did many other miraculous signs in the presence of his disciples, which are not recorded in this book. But these are written that you may believe that Jesus is the Christ, the Son of God, and that by believing you may have life in his name.

When two people who care about each other have been separated for a while, they likely send a stream of letters back and forth. Webbed inside the facts about daily life is a story of love and devotion to the other person.

To find the "good stuff" you would have to wade through the details. If you wanted to find out how the relationship developed, you'd need to study the progression from week to week.

Sometimes that's how it is with the Bible. The events that occurred so long ago don't seem to have any relevance to us today. But if your goal were to trace the relationship between God and his people, from Adam to Jesus, those details would become essential information.

Younger Christians usually want the "good stuff." Later, as they grow in their faith, they'll be more interested in the details that will help them put God's whole plan together. So for now, consider these suggestions:

Get to know Jesus the Christ. Listen to his words. Try to picture what each story and experience is saying, and watch how Christ treats others. John tells us that he wrote his book "so that you will believe that Jesus is the Messiah, the Son of God, and that believing in him you will have life" (John 20:31, TLB). The first four books of the New Testament give four different perspectives to the life of Jesus. Getting to know him should be your first priority.

Next, start reading through some of the smaller letters that Paul, Peter, and John wrote (Paul's letters are everything between Romans and Philemon). If possible, try to use a Bible that can give you some historical information behind each book so that you know the audience it was written to and why it was written.

Try Proverbs next. There are thirty-one of them, so you can read one per day and get through them in a month.

After this, read Genesis, Exodus, Daniel, and Jonah. They offer stories of real people whose problems were not all that different from ours. Learn from their lives so that you don't make the same mistakes they did.

There is no shortcut to the Christian life. We must be disciplined enough to search the Bible to find all the buried treasure that God wants to give to those who will dig deep enough. Have fun!

I'm trying to understand how the Old Testament and the New Testament relate to each other. Which one is more important?

ISAIAH 53:4-6

Surely he took up our infirmities and carried our sorrows, yet we considered him stricken by God, smitten by him, and afflicted. But he was pierced for our transgressions, he was crushed for our iniquities; the punishment that brought us peace was upon him, and by his wounds we are healed. We all, like sheep, have gone astray, each of us has turned to his own way; and the Lord has laid on him the iniquity of us all.

It's not that one is more important than the other. Instead, it's a question of timing.

Imagine being seven years old and your parents sitting you down and telling you all of the rules about driving a car. Not only would you tune them out after about two minutes, but years later when it was time for you to drive, you wouldn't have remembered anything they'd said.

Some important things about living don't need to be said until the right time. Either we aren't smart enough yet to understand it, or we don't really care enough to invest any brain cells in remembering it.

Wise parents have figured out that timing is everything. That's why they didn't give you all the house rules as soon as you could talk. They waited until you were ready, so that you'd *want* to listen, it would *make sense* to you, and you'd *remember* what they said.

The Old Testament was given to us for several reasons. After explaining creation, its main purpose is to point the way to God's solution about the dilemma of man's sin. It tells us not only why we sin (our desire to run our own life), but also what sin is (something so ugly that we can't remove it ourselves).

The Old Testament points directly to Christ as the Savior that we needed. There are dozens of specific verses that foretell the place of Jesus' birth, his sinless life, his death on a cross, his resurrection, and his return. Though it was written from about 1450–400 B.C., it predicted and fulfilled the smallest details about the life of Jesus. This also serves to prove the authority of the Scriptures.

As you study the Bible, you'll see that the Old Testament is what helps the New Testament make sense. An example is found in this passage from Isaiah. For centuries the Hebrews had made yearly sacrifices to take away sin and guilt. The New Testament shows that with the death of Christ, no more sacrifices are needed.

As you read through the Old Testament, you'll often run into foreshadowing like this one in Isaiah. Stories, characteristics of people, prophecies . . . they all point to Jesus. Just as Jesus is the fulfillment of the Old Testament, so is he the fulfillment to all who turn to him.

There are so many things in my life that could pull me away from God. How can I make sure I will always be "good soil"?

LUKE 8:9–15

His disciples asked him what this parable meant. He said, "The knowledge of the secrets of the kingdom of God has been given to you, but to others I speak in parables, so that, 'though seeing, they may not see; though hearing, they may not understand.'

"This is the meaning of the parable: The seed is the word of God. Those along the path are the ones who hear, and then the devil comes and takes away the word from their hearts, so that they may not believe and be saved. Those on the rock are the ones who receive the word with joy when they hear it, but they have no root. They believe for a while, but in the time of testing they fall away. The seed that fell among thorns stands for those who hear, but as they go on their way they are choked by life's worries, riches and pleasures, and they do not mature. But the seed on good soil stands for those with a noble and good heart, who hear the word, retain it, and by persevering produce a crop."

As you get older, you'll discover there is a group of people in this world called insurance salespeople. For a fee, they'll sell you insurance to protect you from financial losses, accidents, catastrophes, or illness. When disaster strikes, the insured person will be reimbursed.

As a Christian, you need an insurance policy to protect you from spiritual disasters. Of course you can't buy this insurance, but God will give you a plan that will "insure" you against your new faith being destroyed.

Skyscrapers must be carefully planned in order for them not to topple when a stiff wind hits. First, a huge hole is dug deep in the ground. Thousands of tons of concrete are poured, steel girders are welded into place, and everything is made to fit according to exact specifications. If the foundation is strong and straight, a sturdy building can be built on it.

The rest of the structure must also be built strong using the best materials. And if they're not fitted together in the right way at the right time, the building will not be as strong as it could have been.

The first phase in your life began when you accepted Christ's forgiveness and became a Christian. "And no one can ever lay any other real foundation than that one we already have—Jesus Christ" (1 Corinthians 3:11, TLB).

The second phase starts with good seed—the Word of God. If you pay close attention to obeying God's Word, asking other Christians to help you understand and apply it, your life in Christ will be strong. "There are various kinds of materials that can be used to build on that foundation. Some use gold and silver and jewels; and some build with sticks, and hay, or even straw!" (1 Corinthians 3:12, TLB).

If you are exposed to teaching that downplays God's Word, it's like building your life with sticks, hay, and straw. It will collapse when problems or persecution from friends or family arise.

The gold, silver, and jewels are the gems you receive when you dig for the treasure in the Bible. God's Word is often referred to as wisdom. "If you want better insight and discernment, and are searching for them as you would for lost money or hidden treasure, then wisdom will be given you, and knowledge of God himself; you will soon learn the importance of reverence for the Lord and of trusting him" (Proverbs 2:3–5, TLB).

Each Christian who comes into your life is building on your foundation. Your goal should be to make sure that all you're hearing is lining up with what the Bible really says. You can do this by praying for direction, asking questions, and finding people who believe as you do that the Bible is our only blueprint that will insure a strong life.

My dad has said some pretty bad things to me over the years. Now that I'm a Christian I know I should forgive him, but I can't. What should I do?

ACTS 3:19–20

Repent, then, and turn to God, so that your sins may be wiped out, that times of refreshing may come from the Lord, and that he may send the Christ, who has been appointed for you—even Jesus.

The gap between knowing you need to forgive someone and actually being able to do it can seem like a vast canyon. You see the other side, but the journey there looks impossible.

Remember the last time the bathroom sink was plugged up with a two-month accumulation of hair? The water would only slowly seep through the molding mass of greasy, soapy yuck. Rarely will a plunger work on gross buildups of stuff in the drain. No amount of suction trying to bring the glob up is strong enough because the clog is too deep.

The next approach usually is to burn away the clog by applying something like Drāno. Sometimes this will work if the buildup is not too severe. The last resort, of course, is to call a plumber. He'll come in with a narrow, hard hose called a "snake" and drill right through the clog until the water is flowing freely.

Unforgiveness is like a clogged drain. Sometimes it's fairly easy to unclog. People hurt us, we let them know they hurt us, they say they're sorry, we forgive them, and the whole episode is usually forgotten.

Unforgiveness from hurts over a number of years is what a drain would look like after years of giving your cat a bath in the sink and never cleaning it! You might as well buy a new sink.

Although it's gross to think about, *our sin* is like a huge hair ball clogging our relationship with God. Until it is removed, we can never really receive anything meaningful from him. Jesus came to unclog our "pipe" so God's love and forgiveness could flow through to us. Though he did nothing wrong, he had to die to do it.

Your dad's sin against you has clogged your relationship. Although you may have done nothing wrong, you've got to unplug the mess so that your relationship can be clean once again. Otherwise the clog will only get worse, and you and your dad won't be free to truly love each other.

God took the initiative with us by humbling himself and forgiving all of our sin. To see the comparison of how much God has forgiven us and how much we must forgive others, read Matthew 18:21–34. You must do the same with any person who wrongs you—especially your dad.

The forgiveness must be from your heart and cannot be dependent upon whether he feels sorry for what he has done. Forgiving someone is a gift only you can offer. You can't make people take a free gift—they must reach out and receive it.

Though the canyon of forgiveness looks deep and treacherous, the reward on the other side is a clear conscience and a renewed friendship.

CHAPTER 31

Is temptation a sin? If it is, I'm sinning all of the time. It seems like thoughts are always coming into my mind to do things that are wrong.

2 PETER 2:9

If this is so, then the Lord knows how to rescue godly men from trials and to hold the unrighteous for the day of judgment, while continuing their punishment.

Temptation isn't a sin, because even Jesus was tempted and we know that he is sinless. (See Matthew 4:1–11 for the story of Satan tempting Jesus in the wilderness.) Temptation isn't a sin; it's the natural consequence of living in this world.

What leads to sin is following the path temptation wants us to take. If taken far enough, the path will cause us to think and do what's wrong.

Though temptation will always be present, we don't have to throw up our hands, wave the white flag, and admit defeat. We have the power to resist because the Holy Spirit lives within us.

God's Word also reminds us how to overcome temptation. 1 Corinthians 10:13 says, "But remember this—the wrong desires that come into your life aren't anything new and different. Many others have faced exactly the same problems before you. And no temptation is irresistible. You can trust God to keep the temptation from becoming so strong that you can't stand up against it, for he has promised this and will do what he says. He will show you how to escape temptation's power so that you can bear up patiently against it" (TLB).

For example, try to figure out where the way of escape occurs in the following story:

You're at school and a friend asks you if you want to spend the night with some other guys and watch videos. You check with your folks and after you assure them there will be no R-rated videos, they give the okay to let you go. Everything is cool . . . so far.

Once you arrive at your friend's house, you look at the stack of videos and notice that half of them are R-rated. You get your friend alone and ask him what the deal is. He says the other guys picked out the videos. Besides, everyone (but you) has seen them before, so he didn't think you'd mind.

Do you not watch the videos in order to obey your parents, or do you say nothing and go along with the group?

Let's say you stay. The next day Dad asks what movies you watched. Now you have to lie to stay out of trouble. So you lie. Unfortunately, Mom spoke with your friend's mom on the phone and found out there *were* R-rated movies at the sleepover. Now you're grounded until age twenty-seven!

Where was the escape hatch to the temptation to disobey your parents? As soon as you found out there were R-rated movies that would be shown, you had two choices. You could have apologized to your friends, called your dad, and had him come pick you up. Or you could have gone to a different part of the house and done something else.

God always provides a way of escape in *every* circumstance. We choose whether to go through the escape hatch or to do things we know are wrong. If we stay close to God, we'll be more likely to resist and do what's right. We don't have to give in.

CHAPTER 32

I hurt inside because I did something rotten to one of my friends. I didn't mean to, but I know I hurt her. I asked God for forgiveness and I tried apologizing to her, but I can tell she hasn't forgiven me. What more can I do to make things right?

ROMANS 12:17–18

Do not repay anyone evil for evil. Be careful to do what is right in the eyes of everybody. If it is possible, as far as it depends on you, live at peace with everyone.

One thing that's hard to do—but is absolutely essential—is to learn the secret of responding to *facts* instead of *feelings*. Our feelings will always betray us. My guess is that you're like every other Christian out there who sometimes doesn't feel like a Christian. Does that mean you aren't one? Absolutely not! Your faith in Christ and his indwelling within you is a fact. The feelings are great, when they come, but this isn't what determines whether we have a relationship with Christ.

So what are the facts in this case?

First, you did something that hurt a friend. Every person who has ever lived has done this. We've got this disease called sin that prevents us from being perfect.

Second, you apologized to your friend and to God. Good work. That's exactly what you should have done.

At this point, you have done everything you can do. And if it's out of your hands, it's in God's hands, right? There is no better place it could be! Leave it there and don't take it back. You can't relive the past, and you can't pay for this sin. Jesus died on the cross to pay for our sin—don't you go doing it yourself by making yourself feel bad.

Now, there are two potential problems to responding correctly to these facts.

1. Was what you did actually unintentional? Only you can answer this. If you asked for forgiveness for something that was unintentional, when in reality it was fairly intentional, this may be the reason you don't sense in your spirit that you're actually forgiven (by God or your friend). In essence, the forgiveness you've sought is incomplete. Search your heart and be brutally honest with yourself. If you know in your heart it was unintentional, your conscience should be clear.

2. The *big* variable in this whole equation is your friend's response to your apology. You needed the gift of forgiveness from her and you didn't get it. Whose fault is that? It's hers, not yours! God always forgives, and since you don't mention whether you feel like God has forgiven you, I'll assume you know this truth. But if your friend cannot respond like God would in this circumstance, there's nothing you can do. Yes, it will hurt. Perhaps for a long time. But it is something out of your control. Time will have to heal this one.

I'm very encouraged by your question. It's obvious you care about people and keeping your relationships clean. This shows a huge amount of maturity, as well as an obvious sensitivity to God's Spirit. It also shows me that whatever mistake you made, you'll likely not make it again.

You'll discover that our mistakes have consequences that we don't like and sometimes are out of our control. It's going to be hard for your friend to trust you again since she feels like she's been burned. Trust is important in all relationships. Your parents will trust you until you consistently break that trust. Then you have to build up a bank account of trust again before it will be like it was. So, too, with friendships. Usually the bank account isn't as large as it is with parents, so when you spend that trust on a poor decision, the vault empties a bit quicker.

Time will prove whether what you had in your friendship can be restored. Try this: Every time you see her, say a quick prayer to God asking him to heal your relationship with her and to help you be a better friend. It sounds like she could use God's Spirit to assist her in her forgiveness, and you could use it so this doesn't happen again.

CHAPTER
33

I have a big question. Who created God? I know that sounds stupid to ask, but I really want to know. And what does it mean when it says we were created in his image?

GENESIS 1:1

In the beginning God created the heavens and the earth. Now the earth was formless and empty, darkness was over the surface of the deep, and the Spirit of God was hovering over the waters.

GENESIS 1:26–27

Then God said, "Let us make man in our image, in our likeness, and let them rule over the fish of the sea and the birds of the air, over the livestock, over all the earth, and over all the creatures that move along the ground." So God created man in his own image, in the image of God he created him; male and female he created them.

JOHN 4:24

God is Spirit, and his worshippers must worship in spirit and in truth.

These are actually great questions. To answer the first, no one created God. He has always been. Unfortunately, in our human, finite minds, we think everything must operate in a natural course. Not so with God. Until Jesus arrived on earth, God wasn't born a human, so he didn't need a mother or a father. And as the passages above confirm, God is spirit, so he is without a body like you and me.

Let me give you something else to think about. If God is spirit, and Genesis says we are created in his image, what does that make us? That's right . . . spirit! What you walk around in is an "earth suit." It's only good for planet earth. If you take it a few miles up, it dies. If you take it underneath the ocean without proper equipment, it dies. It's only good for planet earth! It's a house (or temple, as Paul says in 1 Corinthians). It houses our spirit—our personality, if you will. It's the part of us that Jesus died for because it's the part that lives forever. Our bodies wear out, but our spirit lives forever. Revelation talks about us getting new bodies when we get to heaven.

That's why when you try to make God out to be someone like us who has a mom and dad, well, you just can't. While we're on planet earth, it's tough for us to think of anything different from what we know. Our minds can't comprehend a God so powerful that he could create the universe, our solar system, earth, continents, mountains, animals, people—and then choose to die for his unique creation so we could have a great friendship with him! That, to me, is even more unbelievable than your question. Why would God die for me? Because God is love . . . and he couldn't help but show his love to his people.

CHAPTER 34

I'm not the type of person who can take everything at face value. To be honest, I have a lot of doubts. The whole God and Jesus thing seems so impossible for me to believe that I have to convince myself it's real. What does God think of a doubting believer? I have a hunch he doesn't like them.

GENESIS 2:7

The Lord God formed man from the dust of the ground and breathed into his nostrils the breath of life, and the man became a living being.

If you think God doesn't like doubters, think again. I believe that God welcomes them! Since he created all different varieties of humans, he's not so ignorant to believe a human being that has never seen him before just might have a tough time believing he's really there. God is well aware of our frailties and limitations. You haven't caught him by surprise.

You also said it all seems so impossible that you have to convince yourself to believe. I've thought about that, too. And you're right; it is a little impossible that God would make someone like me—that he would love me enough to die on a cross. He knows how much I willfully sin and that sometimes I silently shake my fist at his lordship whenever I decide to try to follow my own way.

One thing that helps convince me that everything is one hundred percent believable is looking at the facts.

1. He created the earth with incredible order and beauty. Just the process of birth itself is absolutely amazing. Read Psalm 139 today. It describes just exactly what God has done.

2. This world is in a heap of trouble. Most people choose to ignore God, so they do things that are wrong. Wrong behavior has consequences. Nice people sometimes are the recipients of those consequences. Yet this is the world God chose to enter and die for. He knew that many would reject him, but he also knew that the penalty of our sin was something too awful to imagine. He had to do something to kill that penalty. That's why he sent Jesus to die: to kill sin!

3. He loves humans so much that he gave them the power to choose whether to accept or reject his love. He didn't want robots that just obeyed out of helplessness or fear; he wanted real love in return for his.

The questions you are asking are *very* common, especially among teenagers or new Christians. Satan wants to steal the truth away from you to get you to think God doesn't care so you'll turn your back on him. But Satan is a liar, and he's always whispering lies to those who have decided to follow Christ. The only way to shut him up is to know the truth. That means reading the Bible and getting to know God's Son, Jesus. He was the most amazing man who ever walked the earth.

Don't get discouraged. Find some mature Christians to share these real concerns with. They won't think you're stupid. Believe me, they've probably had the same doubts, too.

CHAPTER 35

Does God love everyone the same? A friend of mine says that God loves Christians more than he does non-Christians. Is this true? And what about Christians who constantly give in to temptation? Does God still love them?

JOHN 3:16–18

For God so loved the world that he gave his one and only Son, that whoever believes in him shall not perish but have eternal life. For God did not send his Son into the world to condemn the world, but to save the world through him. Whoever believes in him is not condemned, but whoever does not believe stands condemned already because he has not believed in the name of God's one and only Son.

God loves everyone exactly the same, even non-Christians. He sent Jesus Christ to die on a cross for *everyone*, not just the Christians.

As he expresses his love to those who have trusted in him, he's wise about what he allows them to go through, especially as it relates to temptation. He will only give his kids stuff they can handle.

When God allows Christians to go through temptation, it's like a personal trainer helping an athlete to build muscle. The trainer not only knows how to build strength in each specific muscle, but he knows exactly how much stress to put on that muscle to help strengthen it. A wise trainer wouldn't even consider overtaxing a muscle group before it is ready to handle the stress of more weights. The risk of injury would be too great.

God allows the stress of temptation to come our way for very specific reasons. First, he wants us to strengthen a weak area. And second, he wants to be able to teach us more so he can begin entrusting us with greater gifts. Just as your parents will give you more freedom if they can trust you (a teenager's greatest gift), God wants to trust us. He gains that trust in us by seeing if we will grow to obey him more and more.

Christians who give in to temptation are just as loved by God as those who are able to stand the test. The issue isn't love—it's trust. I know from experience that when I give in to temptation, it means I'm weak and I'm not ready to be trusted as much as I want to be. My spiritual muscles aren't ready.

We are all tempted—temptation is not a sin, but giving in can definitely lead to sin. The miraculous thing, though, is that God is *always* there to forgive our sin and make us clean if we confess it to him. He never says, "Enough is enough." He knows that young (and old) Christians make the same mistakes over and over again. But one day, with discipline and maturity, they move on.

The Christian life isn't one of perfection. It's realizing that we can't be perfect—that's why we need a Savior!

CHAPTER 36

I feel bad asking God for the same things over and over again. And what about asking him for forgiveness for the same sin? I have a habit of gossiping all the time, even though I know it's wrong. He must get annoyed with this!

1 THESSALONIANS 5:17

Pray continually.

I don't know how you're treated at home or with your friends, but God definitely doesn't get tired of hearing from you. He loves it when one of his kids takes the time to sit on his lap and talk. There is nothing better he'd rather do than listen!

You need to realize this about God: He loves us more than any parent or friend could ever love us. He waits, longingly, for us to spend any amount of time with him that we can. We are very special to Him. He made us and died for us, that's how special we are.

Your next question was about committing the same sin of gossip over and over again. All Christians have certain sins they struggle with. Whether you're a new Christian or not, one thing you need to learn is to have more patience with yourself. Just because we recognize something we need to change doesn't mean God will work it out of your life immediately. Habits developed in ignorance are hard to break.

Keep praying about it and have one of your friends who is doing well in this area hold you accountable. Whenever she hears you gossiping, she can mention it to you either at the time (if there's no one else around) or later. We all need accountability.

What you'll find is that once this problem starts to go away (and it will), God will show you another area to begin working on. He is so wise toward us that he doesn't dump all of our faults in front of our face at once and say, "Fix it." Instead, he works with us very patiently until we gradually begin to look more and more like his Son, Jesus. That's his goal.

I heard a speaker talk about God's two wills: perfect and permissive. What was he talking about?

EPHESIANS 5:15–18

*Be very careful, then, how you live—not as unwise but as
wise, making the most of every opportunity, because the days are evil.
Therefore do not be foolish, but understand what the Lord's will is.
Do not get drunk on wine, which leads to debauchery. Instead, be
filled with the Spirit.*

ROMANS 12:2

*Do not conform any longer to the pattern of this world, but
be transformed by the renewing of your mind. Then you will be able
to test and approve what God's will is—his good, pleasing and
perfect will.*

Any time you read about God's will in the New Testament, it's usually referring to holiness or becoming more like Christ. It *is* God's will that we be conformed to the image of his Son (see Romans 8:29). This may be what the man was referring to when he talked about God's perfect will.

God's permissive will is the choices he's given us on this earth. God has given us a will, a "chooser," to be able to make decisions—especially as it pertains to accepting or rejecting his love. We have small decisions to make (what to watch on TV, what music to listen to, what jokes to tell), and big decisions, too (marriage, college, career choices, etc.). God allows us to make these types of decisions on our own.

God has given us a mind to weigh the good and bad of each decision. But he hasn't left us without guidance. He's given his Word as a road map to guide us in the moral implications of each decision. A good example is when a Christian has fallen in love with an unbeliever and is considering marrying him or her. We don't have to wonder whether God thinks this is a good idea or not. He's already told us it isn't (see 2 Corinthians 6:14–18).

Along with his Word, he's put other people in our lives to give us counsel. Parents, pastors, and friends can all be used by God to point us the right way and show us God's will.

Discerning God's will is a challenge you'll face your whole life. It's actually a fun challenge, too. Life would get boring if we knew what the future held in every circumstance.

Two things are sure: (1) God's will for us is to learn what it means to become more like Jesus—making the right moral choices—and (2) we need to consult his Word and other people to help us make the big decisions that will affect our lives.

CHAPTER 38

I have a friend who thinks that someone made up Christianity to keep people in line. How do we really know that Islam or Buddhism isn't the right religion and Christianity is the wrong one?

JOHN 14:6

Jesus answered, "I am the way and the truth and the life.
No one comes to the Father except through me."

Did you know that Christians are the only people of faith who say their leader is still alive? Buddhists don't think Buddha is alive, Moslems don't say Mohammed is still alive, and Jews don't say Moses is still alive. Yet Christians have the audacity to say that Jesus died but rose from the dead. That either makes us crazy, liars . . . or people who have found the truth. There is no middle ground.

Jesus wasn't just a good teacher. He was either God (as he said he was) or a nut. Someone who compares himself with God is either right or should be put away. Personally, I have chosen to believe he is still alive. Why? A number of reasons:

- The authority of the Bible. Nowhere in literature could forty-two different authors write sixty-six "books" over a period of fifteen hundred years without any major discrepancies.
- There are more than three hundred prophecies in the

Old Testament about the Messiah, Jesus, and Jesus fulfilled every one!

- Jesus was a real person who claimed he was God, and his actions backed up his word. Rarely will someone die for something they know to be a lie. But because he *knew* he was God, and knew his mission, he wasn't afraid to face the Cross.

- The experiences of millions of believers, as well as my own experience after living separate from him the first eighteen years of my life. My own relationship with God, though it can't be proven "scientifically," can be proven by changes in my actions and attitudes about others.

Have you ever sincerely believed you were right about something but then found out later you were sincerely wrong? I sure have. While people throughout the world are wholeheartedly following the gods of their culture, Christianity isn't a faith that asks you to throw your mind out the window. It makes logical sense, historical sense, and personal sense.

It may be that your friend is after attention, or perhaps he just wants to run his own life and not worry about which religion to follow. If he is genuinely seeking the right answer, he will eventually find it in Jesus Christ. Otherwise, he won't. Keep praying for him and challenge him to check things out. Encourage him to go to the Bible if he's really looking for the right answers. The fruit of Islam or Buddhism and other religions are evident. He won't find a leader who is still alive among those religions, and he won't find a relationship with God. He may find a religious code it says to follow in order to gain God's favor, but he'll miss knowing God in a personal way.

CHAPTER 39

I'm about ready to graduate from school and I sense God is asking me to become a missionary. I'm open to God's call, but sometimes I'm a bit confused how to determine if it's God calling me ... or something else. How do I know if God's calling me to be a missionary?

1 SAMUEL 3:4–10

Then the Lord called Samuel.

Samuel answered, "Here I am." And he ran to Eli and said, "Here I am; you called me."

But Eli said, "I did not call; go back and lie down." So he went and lay down.

Again the Lord called, "Samuel!" And Samuel got up and went to Eli and said, "Here I am; you called me."

"My son," Eli said, "I did not call; go back and lie down."

Now Samuel did not yet know the Lord; the word of the Lord had not yet been revealed to him.

The Lord called Samuel a third time, and Samuel got up and went to Eli and said, "Here I am; you called me."

*Then Eli realized that the Lord was calling the boy. So Eli
told Samuel, "Go and lie down, and if he calls you, say, 'Speak,
Lord, for your servant is listening.' " So Samuel went and lay down
in his place.*

*The Lord came and stood there, calling as at other times,
"Samuel, Samuel!"*

Then Samuel said, "Speak, for your servant is listening."

This is a huge question that probably needs more space than I can devote in this book. Though I wish each person's call were as obvious as it was for Samuel, most of the time it isn't. But let me get you started.

I believe God's call starts with a burden for a certain group or a certain type of people. Your heart has to break for their situation. For me, it was for non-Christian teens. Because I was one before I became a Christian in college, I had an aching heart for those who were like me. My burden for this age group, I'm certain, was something God put there. Why? I had been sincerely praying about what he wanted to do with my life.

Personally, I believe God gives a burden to every believer for some segment of society. It's just that some Christians choose to cover it up or they never ask God to increase it and show them even more convincingly what it is. They become selfish, consumer-oriented people who can't imagine life without four bedrooms, two baths, and a shopping mall less than fifteen minutes away.

Once we have the burden, then comes the testing. God will give you the opportunity to act on that burden. He does that either through small-step experiences (mission trips, campus evangelism, etc.) or through training (languages). For instance, if you have a heart for the poor people of Honduras, but your skin gets constant rashes from the heat (after going on a short-term experience), and you just can't learn the language, God may be letting you know he has something else in mind.

The key is availability, not just ability. If you let God know that you're serious about pursuing the privilege of ministry, he is faithful to confirm his will in you. There is no higher calling than to be selected by God to work full time for him. He doesn't take it lightly. Keep praying and ask your friends, parents, and youth leaders to pray also.

If God is calling you to be a missionary, he'll confirm it in many ways:

1. Your burden for the lost will continue to grow.

2. Others will affirm your ability to reach out to the lost.

3. People who are praying for you will give you godly counsel when the time comes to make decisions about your training.

If I were you, I'd do these minimums while you're finishing school—and waiting for God to confirm his call:

- Study your Bible—a lot!
- Continue to share your faith as God gives opportunity in school. Don't be a geek about it, just be natural.
- Ask a group of prayer warriors to pray that your life won't be stained by sin. So many things can go wrong during the teenage years—there are so *many* temptations—that you don't want a trainload of regret to rob you of the zeal God has given you.

Work on these main priorities, and you will do well.

CHAPTER 40

My dad says that since he's never hurt anyone, he's good enough to make it into heaven. I'm starting to agree with him. God won't send people who live good lives to hell, will he?

PSALM 14:1-3

The fool says in his heart, "There is no God." They are corrupt, their deeds are vile; there is no one who does good. The Lord looks down from heaven on the sons of men to see if there are any who understand, any who seek God. All have turned aside, they have together become corrupt; there is no one who does good, not even one.

Teachers have developed two systems for grading their students' performance. First, there is the A, B, C, D, and F method, better known as the "curve." Put simply, fifty percent of a particular class will score above the average, fifty percent will score below. Often those who score below the average still have the chance to pass. That's why students seem to like this system best.

Then there is the pass/fail method. Either you scored the right amount or came to enough classes, or you didn't. There is less room for error.

Most people would like to believe that God grades on a curve. Though ninety percent of the people won't get *A*s, at least sixty percent will pass. All you have to do to pass is not kill anyone, not steal, mind your own business, and wait for heaven.

Unfortunately, God doesn't grade that way. Here's why.

First, the passage you just read is clear. There isn't anyone who is good. Not one! All of us have strayed away. This doesn't mean we're all murderers. It means our hearts are stained with the sin of Adam—the desire to be god in our lives and run them ourselves. No one has a pure heart (see Luke 18:18–26 for a great illustration).

Second, think how unfair that standard really is. It doesn't leave any room for someone who has really messed up their life to be accepted by God and go to heaven.

Third, the curve system tells people that their *behavior* determines their eternal destiny. If you do more good works to counterbalance the bad stuff, then you're in. Many cults base their religion on how many good works they do. It somehow makes heaven seem more attainable. But having to do good works to get God's favor is just wasted effort. How many people would really qualify if they had to rely on their life to impress God?

God is clear on *one* method of salvation. In his wisdom, he gave everyone the opportunity to go to heaven—by faith, not works. All a person has to do is believe that Christ paid the penalty for sin and rose again from the dead.

"Because of his kindness you have been saved through trusting Christ. And even trusting is not of yourselves; it too is a gift from God. Salvation is not a reward for the good we have done, so none of us can take any credit for it" (Ephesians 2:8–9, TLB).

Most people say this is too simple. But that's the whole idea! God isn't trying to make it tough on us. He wants us to be with him forever!

Throughout your life you'll run into people who believe simply living a good life means heaven awaits. A good life is important to point people to a holy God, but it will not buy you a ticket to heaven. Jesus Christ has already paid for that ticket!

CHAPTER 41

There aren't very many Christians at my school, and I'm kind of embarrassed about admitting I am one. Do I have to come out and let the whole world know I've become a Christian?

LUKE 22:54-62

Then seizing him, they led him away and took him into the house of the high priest. Peter followed at a distance. But when they had kindled a fire in the middle of the courtyard and had sat down together, Peter sat down with them. A servant girl saw him seated there in the firelight. She looked closely at him and said, "This man was with him."

But he denied it. "Woman, I don't know him," he said.

A little later someone else saw him and said, "You also are one of them."

"Man, I am not!" Peter replied.

About an hour later another asserted, "Certainly this fellow was with him, for he is a Galilean."

Peter replied, "Man, I don't know what you're talking about!" Just as he was speaking, the rooster crowed. The Lord turned and looked straight at Peter. Then Peter remembered the word the Lord had spoken to him: "Before the rooster crows today, you will disown me three times." And he went outside and wept bitterly.

Some teenage guys and girls wear letter jackets that tell the world they're athletes. The jacket also identifies them with a specific school, sport, and group of athletes. Those who wear these jackets have accomplished something, and they want other people to know.

Identifying yourself as a Christian, however, isn't always popular. Peter found that out when he was confronted by the people who were trying to get warm around the fire. Though he had walked with Jesus for three years and was likely one of Christ's best friends, he denied even knowing who Jesus was!

Peter was afraid, he was embarrassed, and he wasn't really sure he wanted the world to know about his association with Jesus. But something happened during the next two months that convinced him he would never be ashamed of Jesus again. (You can read about what he did in the first four chapters of the book of Acts.)

When you're a new Christian, it's hard to identify yourself with Jesus because you don't know him very well. It's like striking up a friendship with the new kid at school. Although you want to be his friend, sometimes you hold back because you aren't sure how popular he's going to be. Some people would even quit talking to a person just because he's not in the popular crowd.

Jesus understands our fears about identifying ourselves with him. In some situations it's tough to admit we're one of his followers. Though he is patient and understanding about our insecurity, I can imagine it kind of disappoints him a little, too.

Most new and younger Christians go through a process to get to the point where they aren't embarrassed about admitting they're believers in Christ. For some people it takes years; for others it may happen the moment they believe in him. Something clicks that absolutely convinces them that Jesus Christ really is alive. It could be the feeling of being forgiven; it could be a miraculous answer to prayer; it could be that someone they know has changed so much that only God could have done the changing. For some, it might be a quiet realization that the Bible is accurate and everything Jesus said about himself is true.

God doesn't expect you to get on the P.A. system at school as soon as it happens and make the "big announcement." He expects you to be ready in case anyone asks you about your faith.

"Quietly trust yourself to Christ your Lord and if anybody asks why you believe as you do, be ready to tell him, and do it in a gentle and respectful way" (1 Peter 3:15, TLB).

I hear Christians talk a lot about God's will. Has God planned out everything I'll ever do?

PROVERBS 16:1

To man belong the plans of the heart, but from the Lord comes the reply of the tongue.

Follow these instructions: Put your right hand straight up in the air. Now place your index finger in your left ear (come on, your left ear). Now take two fingers and put them in a wall socket.

Who controlled your hand and fingers?

Tough question. Especially if you were silly enough to do what was asked. But we know from experience that people give us instructions, and we choose either to obey or not.

The question, however, is who has control—you or God? This has been debated for centuries, and the discussion can get quite complicated. For now, let's keep it as simple as possible.

First, you must know that God loves you too much to force you to obey him. He doesn't force us to follow him. He also doesn't force you to ask his Son, Jesus, into your life, but he makes it clear that it's God's will for everyone to be saved. "He isn't really being slow about his promised return, even though it sometimes seems that way. But he is waiting, for the good reason that he is not willing that any should perish, and he is giving more time for sinners to repent" (2 Peter 3:9, TLB).

So what is God's will for us?

First, it's to know him. "And this is the way to have eternal life—by knowing you, the only true God, and Jesus Christ, the one you sent to earth!" (John 17:3, TLB).

Second, it's to help others. "For we are God's workmanship, created in Christ Jesus to do good works, which God prepared in advance for us to do" (Ephesians 2:10).

Third, it's to be filled with the Holy Spirit. "So be careful how you act; these are difficult days. Don't be fools; be wise: make the most of every opportunity you have for doing good. Don't act thoughtlessly, but try to find out and do whatever the Lord wants you to. Don't drink too much wine, for many evils lie along that path; be filled instead with the Holy Spirit, and controlled by Him" (Ephesians 5:15–18, TLB). By allowing God to fill you, you are really saying, "God, take my will and help me to do what you want."

There are many other specific things, of course, that God requires of us as we grow in our relationship with him. If, however, you focus your efforts on these, God will reveal the others to you in his perfect timing.

CHAPTER 43

My church regularly does something called "Communion." What is it supposed to do for me?

LUKE 24:30-35

When he was at the table with them, he took bread, gave thanks, broke it and began to give it to them. Then their eyes were opened and they recognized him, and he disappeared from their sight. They asked each other, "Were not our hearts burning within us while he talked with us on the road and opened the Scriptures to us?"

They got up and returned at once to Jerusalem. There they found the Eleven and those with them, assembled together and saying, "It is true! The Lord has risen and has appeared to Simon." Then the two told what had happened on the way, and how Jesus was recognized by them when he broke the bread.

Have you ever saved something from a special event because you wanted to remember how great a certain moment was? A ticket stub? A card? A trophy?

Ask your parents to take you through their scrapbooks and memory boxes sometime. They'll say things like, "And this is the varsity letter I won my senior year for swimming," or, "Here is the ring box that contained the ring your father gave me the day he proposed."

Certain items help us remember special moments in our lives.

When Jesus knew that he was about to die, be raised, and

return to heaven, he wanted to leave his followers something tangible to remember him by. He could have left a physical item like a robe or cup. But he was smart enough to know that people would begin to worship the object instead of God. So instead he left a ceremony, something to do.

He gave Christians a word picture of what he did on the cross for all time. He shed his blood, though he was innocent. His body was broken, though we deserved the punishment he bore. Communion (the Lord's Supper, Eucharist) is that act.

The passage says that Jesus was "recognized as he was breaking the bread" (verse 35). Communion helps us recognize who Jesus is and that he's with us as we worship. And because believers throughout the world celebrate Communion, it's a unifying act.

"For this is what the Lord himself has said about his Table, and I have passed it on to you before: That on the night when Judas betrayed him, the Lord Jesus took bread, and when he had given thanks to God for it, he broke it and gave it to his disciples and said, 'Take this and eat it. This is my body, which is given for you. Do this to remember me.' In the same way, he took the cup of wine after supper, saying, 'This cup is the new agreement between God and you that has been established and set in motion by my blood. Do this in remembrance of me whenever you drink it.' For every time you eat this bread and drink this cup you are re-telling the message of the Lord's death, that he has died for you. Do this until he comes again" (1 Corinthians 11:23–26, TLB).

Every time we take Communion we retell the message of Christ's death and we are reminded that he is going to return someday to take us to heaven.

Christians will always need those reminders. There are too many distractions that cause us to lose our focus on what really matters in this life. Communion briefly reminds us that real life revolves not around us, but around one incredible act of love at a certain time in history.

This world has a lot of unhappiness. Rotten things go on all of the time. Does God really care? What's the point of it all?

JOHN 11:32–35

When Mary reached the place where Jesus was and saw him, she fell at his feet and said, "Lord, if you had been here, my brother would not have died."

When Jesus saw her weeping, and the Jews who had come along with her also weeping, he was deeply moved in spirit and troubled. "Where have you laid him?" he asked.

"Come and see, Lord," they replied.

Jesus wept.

There are bad things that happen, and then there are tragedies. At some time in life everyone will experience both of these. Let's look at bad things first.

The person who flunked a math test had something bad happen to him. Did he learn that it's important to keep up with assignments and study before a test? Hopefully.

A ten-year-old boy races out from behind a parked car and is nearly hit by a truck that couldn't see him. He's scared to death, realizing that he could have been killed! Did he learn a lesson about not darting into the street? He better have; he may not get another chance!

In each case the person probably was not happy about what happened. But *each situation in life, good or bad, is a learning experience.*

Does God care that we learn important lessons about studying and safety? He cares very much!

Ask your folks what the five worst things are that have happened to them in their lives. Then ask what they have learned from these bad experiences. Finally, ask them if they were thankful that these occurred. Going through tough times is truly bad if you don't learn something when it's over.

Now let's discuss tragedy.

Unfortunately, no one is immune to what we believe is the ultimate tragedy—death. It's the timing of death (especially for those who die young), and how awful it can be (like an innocent victim at the hands of a drunk driver), that makes us wonder if God really cares.

When Adam and Eve disobeyed God in the Garden of Eden, their punishment was separation from his presence. This incident also set in motion the life cycle, which ends in death. But the good news is that Jesus Christ's death on the cross killed death! Not physical death, but spiritual death for all those who receive his gift of forgiveness.

The curse that Adam brought the human race was physical death. Since that time, *man* has invented ways to make death happen in some pretty ugly ways (nuclear bombs, lung cancer, AIDS, and many others). None of these forms of physical death was God's plan for his creation.

God sees the big picture and realizes that spiritual death is far worse than physical death. That's why he focused all of his attention on taking care of the penalty of our sin—spiritual death (see Romans 6:23).

Another part of the big picture God sees is how tragedy can be used if we look to him to show us the purpose behind it. "And we know that all that happens to us is working for our good if we love God and are fitting into his plans" (Romans 8:28, TLB).

Although God is not in heaven pushing buttons to make people die young, he can use *any* situation for good. And remember, whatever happens to you, God cares. He loves you and wants to work out his purposes in your life.

CHAPTER 45

Some Christians I deeply respected and cared for have hurt me very much. This girl and her parents—Christians who have gone to church forever—hurt me a lot. I still love these people, but I can't get over how such strong Christians could do such a thing. What will help me regain my respect for them?

ACTS 15:36–40

Some time later Paul said to Barnabas, "Let us go back and visit the brothers in all the towns where we preached the word of the Lord and see how they are doing." Barnabas wanted to take John, also called Mark, with them, but Paul did not think it wise to take him, because he had deserted them in Pamphylia and had not continued with them in the work. They had such a sharp disagreement that they parted company. Barnabas took Mark and sailed for Cyprus, but Paul chose Silas and left, commended by the brothers to the grace of the Lord.

Since I don't have enough information about how you were hurt, I can do nothing to explain the actions of this older Christian who hurt you. I do know, however, that people—even God's people—can be heartless at times. In their immaturity in dealing with others, some will say and do things that do not need to be done.

You need to remember this about Christian people: Though their spirits have been redeemed, they're still trapped in a human body. Mistakes are inevitable.

Regarding your own sense of hurt and betrayal, I'm not sure there really are words to comfort. Jesus said, "In this life you will have tribulation. . . ." He is so right!

All I can ask is that you resist the temptation to look at everything that happens to you as something you can't learn from. There have been dozens of negative experiences in my life that I didn't understand why they happened. But with the passage of time, these experiences have come back to teach me things about life, eternity, or helping others. We must take each episode in life and not judge it by the effects in the here and now, but rather by asking, "What can God teach me through this?"

The passage above describes a situation in the early church that I'm sure left people scratching their heads. Paul and Barnabas were great friends and fellow missionaries, but they couldn't agree about Mark's usefulness. They parted ways. Their disagreement, however, meant two teams of missionaries were sent to two different parts of the world. And though we never hear from Barnabas again, later in life, Paul and Mark are reconciled (see 2 Timothy 4:11).

I have found that those who look at unfortunate experiences more optimistically, as learning and growing experiences, are those whom God uses the most. It's not that they're immune to the initial hurts, but rather they are willing to wait for the big picture to come to pass before they pass judgment on whether a certain experience that happened to them was actually good or bad. Give yourself—and God—time to work through this hurt.

CHAPTER 46

My parents are getting a divorce, I'm not doing well in school, and my friends aren't sticking by me. How can God possibly use all of the problems I've been facing?

ROMANS 8:28

And we know that in all things God works for the good of those who love him, who have been called according to his purpose.

I wasn't a Christian during those years when my family self-destructed. We moved countless times, and I really became scarred for life by the choices I made trying to make up for the love and attention I wasn't getting from my family. My parents were alcoholics, and I used to smoke dope with my dad. I was headed for a lifetime of pain without Christ.

After I became a Christian (Oct. 6, 1974!), God slowly showed me that even though he didn't cause the situation I was forced to live through, he could use it for his good—if I let him. The passage above is a clear promise—with a condition. I had to love him and follow him for me to know what good could come out of the junk I went through.

These past years God has used this life that was headed nowhere to help . . . thousands. Unbelievable! No one I knew in high school would have ever thought my life would have headed in a positive direction. And it's all because I allowed Jesus to take my pain and use it to empathize with others. He can do that with you, too—if you let him.

The condition? Love God with all your heart. Don't blame him or be bitter toward him because of the circumstances *people* have taken you through. People have a tendency to let you down. Draw close to him by praying, reading, and, when you can, helping others who may be going through the same type of situation you've faced. Only then will you be able to see the purpose behind the struggles.

If and when you finally get settled, look for an older Christian who will walk with you and love you unconditionally like God does. You probably need a good example to look to—I'll pray you find one.

If I don't read the Bible, does God still try to talk to me?

NUMBERS 22:27-31

When the donkey saw the angel of the Lord, she lay down under Balaam, and he was angry and beat her with his staff. Then the Lord opened the donkey's mouth, and she said to Balaam, "What have I done to you to make you beat me these three times?"

Balaam answered the donkey, "You have made a fool of me! If I had a sword in my hand, I would kill you right now."

The donkey said to Balaam, "Am I not your own donkey, which you have always ridden, to this day? Have I been in the habit of doing this to you?"

"No," he said.

Then the Lord opened Balaam's eyes, and he saw the angel of the Lord standing in the road with his sword drawn. So he bowed low and fell face down.

The Bible is our main source for direct communication from God. Everything essential he wanted to say to his followers he's put in the Bible. But God often uses more than his Word to teach us about walking with him, learning about life, and hearing from him. He uses your parents, pastor, even friends and teachers who aren't Christians! If God can speak through a donkey, he can speak through anything or anyone. The key is being able to discern what the life lessons are he's trying to teach you.

I can still hear my dad speak at times though he has now passed away. What can I hear? Unfortunately, not much that truly encourages me to live a godly life. But because of the falseness of what he tried to tell me, I can hear more clearly the truth of what God says. The fruit of his life showed me his words were not correct. His words and (often) poor counsel taught me life lessons I'll never forget.

Have you ever noticed another classmate put someone down? And then did you see the reaction of the one who was hurt? If you noticed these things—and learned from them—God has spoken to you in a life lesson. If you're looking, you'll hear God's voice in unexpected places.

CHAPTER 48

When I was at a Christian camp last summer, everyone seemed to swear. It got so bad that I even started in. What does God think about Christians who swear?

MARK 7:20-23

He went on: "What comes out of a man is what makes him 'unclean.' For from within, out of men's hearts, come evil thoughts, sexual immorality, theft, murder, adultery, greed, malice, deceit, lewdness, envy, slander, arrogance and folly. All these evils come from inside and make a man 'unclean.'"

EPHESIANS 4:29-32

Do not let any unwholesome talk come out of your mouths, but only what is helpful for building others up according to their needs, that it may benefit those who listen. And do not grieve the Holy Spirit of God, with whom you were sealed for the day of redemption. Get rid of all bitterness, rage and anger, brawling and slander, along with every form of malice. Be kind and compassionate to one another, forgiving each other, just as in Christ God forgave you.

Swearing is only part of the problem; it's also a symptom of something deeper.

First, one reason people (including adults) swear is they're insecure. Swearing in order to fit in with a specific group is a perfect example. If everyone else is saying certain words, a person will feel left out if they don't join in. Unfortunately, insecurity is very common during the teen years. Friends are more important than anything else. And if you don't have them, you'll feel out of it. That's why teens will usually go along with the group instead of standing for what they know is right. This may be where you are.

Your swearing is a dilemma when the more you do it, the less guilty you feel. It becomes an acceptable way to communicate, and since God hasn't hit you with a lightning bolt, it must not be too bad, right? Well . . .

Second, swearing shows a disrespect for others and God. It really is sin (reread the passages above). Minor, perhaps, but if God talks about it (and he does a lot through the book of Proverbs), he knows it's not cool. Especially since swearing is often directed at someone and devalues him or her as God's special creation. That's definitely not cool.

Am I worried about this for you? Not too much. I think you know what is right, and I think you would do the right thing if you felt you wouldn't be a social outcast at camp if you took a stand. But that might be too much to ask of you right now. For some kids, that price is too high to pay. One day, though, I hope you'll allow the Lord to give you the strength to make a stand. Not in a self-righteous way, but in a way that others would want to follow. Not much good can come from a foul mouth, as I think you know. You're the one who controls your mouth. It's your choice either to swear or offer words that encourage others.

I've heard so many different opinions on what God is really like that I'm beginning to wonder if someone can ever know. Is there any way to know for sure?

HEBREWS 1:1-3

In the past God spoke to our forefathers through the prophets at many times and in various ways, but in these last days he has spoken to us by his Son, whom he appointed heir of all things, and through whom he made the universe. The Son is the radiance of God's glory and the exact representation of his being, sustaining all things by his powerful word. After he had provided purification for sins, he sat down at the right hand of the Majesty in heaven.

Imagine you're in a department store browsing through the game section. Within this area are hundreds of games along with dozens of boxes of puzzles. You notice about ten of the puzzle boxes are the same size.

Suddenly, a bolt of mayhem enters your mind. "What if I switched the tops on all of the boxes of puzzles?" You laugh as you imagine people bringing the puzzle home, opening it, and trying to match pieces to the wrong picture! Though it sounds like fun, your conscience gets the better of you, so you nix the whole fiendish idea.

People throughout the world are trying to put the "God puzzle" together. Their main dilemma is they are often trying to match the pieces to the wrong picture!

God isn't trying to hide. He has clearly shown the world what he is like. He didn't part the clouds, put a heavenly megaphone to his lips, and *tell* us what he was like. He came down to earth and *showed* us.

Jesus said it plainly, "I and the Father are one" (John 10:30).

Even when he was asked point-blank by Philip, he was straightforward in his reply. "Don't you even yet know who I am, Philip, even after all this time I have been with you? Anyone who has seen me has seen the Father! So why are you asking to see him?" (John 14:9, TLB).

It doesn't get more obvious than that to know what God is like. All you have to do is look intently at the life of Jesus.

People get their God pictures from TV preachers; friends who say they believe in God but never act like it; something they heard their grandma say eight years ago; coaches who pray before a game, then swear the paint off of the walls at half time; a street preacher screaming out "hell and damnation"; and elsewhere. These pictures of God aren't anything like him. They don't look like the loving God you're supposed to get to know. That's why it's so important to not settle for hearsay when it comes to finding out what God is like.

Though there is much beauty in the world that points to God, a wise man once said, "You can see God in nature, but you can only see the nature of God in Jesus."

CHAPTER 50

I notice people at school give some Christians a pretty tough time, especially in class. This kind of scares me off from ever letting anyone know I'm a believer. Any suggestions?

ACTS 7:54–59

When they heard this, they were furious and gnashed their teeth at him. But Stephen, full of the Holy Spirit, looked up to heaven and saw the glory of God, and Jesus standing at the right hand of God. "Look," he said, "I see heaven open and the Son of Man standing at the right hand of God."

At this they covered their ears and, yelling at the top of their voices, they all rushed at him, dragged him out of the city and began to stone him. Meanwhile, the witnesses laid their clothes at the feet of a young man named Saul.

While they were stoning him, Stephen prayed, "Lord Jesus, receive my spirit."

Though no one likes rejection, it comes with being a Christian. Our lives and beliefs go against the flow of the rest of the world. Growing closer to God will naturally make you grow farther away from the world.

Imagine flying in a helicopter over the earth and being able to see all of history from beginning to end. You'd understand so much more because you could see the whole picture. Unfortunately, only God enjoys that luxury. We have to live on this earth without being able to see everything in the future.

Stephen made a stand for Christ that cost him much more than rejection from a few friends. It cost him his life. But if Stephen could have known what his death would accomplish, he would have died smiling.

A man named Saul held the coats of those who threw the rocks that killed Stephen. Immediately after this, he received permission to go and round up other Christians from faraway cities in order to bring *them* back to be killed, as well!

It was on the way to one of these cities that Christ personally confronted Saul. Though it's not said, Saul likely remembered the way Stephen died. Saul's heart was broken, and he became a devoted follower of Jesus.

Saul—later renamed Paul—didn't just become a Sunday-morning-pew-sitter type of follower. He went on to travel the entire Roman world and share the good news about Christ. He also wrote nearly half of the New Testament! Stephen's rejection helped bring Paul to Christ.

People *are* watching you and other Christians at school. They are seeing how you respond to rejection and verbal abuse. Within those crowded halls are people who want to believe in something true, something worth living for, no matter what the cost. And when they find it, they may make an incredible impact in their world for Christ.

What do they learn from watching you?

I have a friend asking questions about God. Should I give her a Bible and invite her to church?

HEBREWS 4:12

For the word of God is living and active. Sharper than any double-edged sword, it penetrates even to dividing soul and spirit, joints and marrow; it judges the thoughts and attitudes of the heart.

Most definitely give her a Bible. But how about a New Testament for starters? It's smaller and not so intimidating. You need to show her how to read it, too. Explain the difference between the first four books (the Gospels), Acts, Paul's letters, the other smaller letters, and Revelation. (If you're not sure, talk to your parents or your youth leader.) You want to make sure she has a Bible that will be "reader friendly."

Should you invite her to church? Well, that depends on your church. If there are a lot of confusing things going on in the service that would make her feel uncomfortable, I'd say no. But if it were just singing contemporary choruses, some special music, and a message from someone she can relate to, then it would be a great idea.

God uses his Word and what goes on in church in remarkable ways. But what will probably be the best thing for her is to get her into relationships with young Christians and the adult youth sponsors. When your youth group does something fun, even if it doesn't have a spiritual goal, invite her and let her rub shoulders with other believers. And whenever she's invited, always make sure she knows exactly what's going to happen. Don't ever take her to something where she's going to feel uncomfortable; don't misrepresent what's going to go on. If you know there's going to be an invitation for people to become Christians, tell her ahead of time. That way she won't feel pressured, surprised, or betrayed.

Stick with her! You're the person God has put in her life right now. Be the influencer, not the influenced.

My grandma has been a Christian for forty years.

She has faced so much trouble during those years

I can't believe it. Two husbands and one child

have died, and her house recently burned down.

Why would God allow so much hardship to come

into one person's life?

JAMES 1:2–4

Consider it pure joy, my brothers, whenever you face trials of
many kinds, because you know that the testing of your faith develops
perseverance. Perseverance must finish its work so that you may be
mature and complete, not lacking anything.

No doubt you've seen weight lifters on TV or have friends who work out with weights. The goal of lifting weights, of course, is to develop your muscles and make them stronger. Do you know how that's done? Your muscles grow stronger by being constantly broken down! Through the repetition of lifting, a strain is built up that at first causes someone to feel weak. In the long run, however, it makes him or her strong.

Like a muscle, faith grows stronger when it's exercised. That's why this passage says to be happy when facing difficult trials and temptations.

One of God's goals for us is to constantly learn to trust

him more. When Christians ask God for more faith, they are really asking for more trials. God knows that only through this kind of "exercise" can their faith be strengthened. The end result, James says, is that we will be "ready for anything, strong in character, full and complete" (TLB).

Another reason for trials and problems is found in 2 Corinthians 1:3–5—helping others. "What a wonderful God we have—he is the Father of our Lord Jesus Christ, the source of every mercy, and the one who so wonderfully comforts and strengthens us in our hardships and trials. And why does he do this? So that when others are troubled, needing our sympathy and encouragement, we can pass on to them this same help and comfort God has given us. You can be sure that the more we undergo sufferings for Christ, the more he will shower us with his comfort and encouragement" (TLB).

Helping someone else is probably the last thing we're thinking about when we are going through problems. But God knows that by allowing us to go through trials, we will be all the more able to pass along comfort and encouragement to others when they're facing difficult times.

There was a basketball coach who once told his players, "Don't worry when I'm yelling at you, start worrying when I stop yelling!" What he was saying was, "If I quit yelling at you, I've given up on you."

Some Christians are glad they rarely face any problems. Unfortunately, they won't have the opportunity to see their character grow stronger. And they won't receive the joy that comes when they help others.

CHAPTER 53

Although I recently became a Christian, I'm having second thoughts. I feel like I'll miss out on a lot of fun during my teenage years. Can't I wait until later to live for Christ?

ECCLESIASTES 11:9–12:2

Be happy, young man, while you are young, and let your heart give you joy in the days of your youth. Follow the ways of your heart and whatever your eyes see, but know that for all these things God will bring you to judgment. So then, banish anxiety from your heart and cast off the troubles of your body, for youth and vigor are meaningless.

Remember your Creator in the days of your youth, before the days of trouble come and the years approach when you will say, "I find no pleasure in them"—before the sun and the light and the moon and the stars grow dark, and the clouds return after the rain.

A speaker once told of having a dream. The location was hell, and the demons were trying to think of ways to stop people from accepting Christ. Each demon brought an idea to Satan and was given approval to try it. The ideas included the typical ones people often think are responsible for turning others away: drugs, sexual temptations, intellectualism, money, fame, and status. These ideas were all tried by various demons, but they were never completely effective at keeping people from turning to Christ.

Finally, one demon laid forth a plan that was surprising to all. He said they should tell people that believing the Bible and following Christ was the right thing to do, and to tell them that being a committed believer was the only way to live life. "But," he concluded, "tell them to do it—*tomorrow*!"

That has become Satan's strategy. And for many people tomorrow never comes! Though you feel like you'll miss out on the fun, Satan knows that "good times" don't last. Most of what the world pursues is shallow and meaningless (even though it sometimes feels fun for a time). The delay tactic in full use today works like novocain. It numbs people and keeps them from turning to the truth once they hear it.

We are creatures of habit. Almost everything we know we learned by repetition—reading, writing, math, speech, and manners. It comes from years of doing the same thing over and over again.

Our thoughts about God are the same way. If when we're young we believe that we can play now and get committed later, we fulfill Satan's strategy. Thought patterns become habits, habits become actions, actions become beliefs, and beliefs determine our eternity!

If your definition of fun is to make sure God takes his rightful place behind the four walls of a church instead of your heart, then, yes, you can push God away. (Read the second half of Luke 15 for a great story on a young man who did just that.)

Please realize, however, that youth is a gift. You are only young once. More regret comes out of those years than in any other period in a person's life.

To live life to the fullest, we need to follow God. Not in fear that he wants to take away your fun, but in faith that he wants to make your life into something you can be proud of. Life begins for people the moment they realize that the world doesn't revolve around *them*, but around God who made the world and all that is in it.

CHAPTER 54

I have done some pretty awful things in my life—things that other kids never even think about doing. I really don't see how God could forgive me for what I've done.

JEREMIAH 17:9-10

The heart is deceitful above all things and beyond cure. Who can understand it? "I the Lord search the heart and examine the mind, to reward a man according to his conduct, according to what his deeds deserve."

Recognition of wrong is ninety percent of the battle.

Usually, people who build up years of wrong actions have also built a shell around their hearts. The shell protects them from feeling guilty about something they've done wrong. As the shell gets harder and thicker around their hearts, they continue the spiral downward toward doing more and more things that are wrong.

Somewhere in our lives, God gives each of us a peek inside our hearts and lets us take a good look. Jeremiah, a prophet of God, received his peek early in life and came to this conclusion: "The heart is the most deceitful thing there is, and desperately wicked. No one can really know how bad it is! Only the Lord knows! He searches all hearts and examines deepest motives so he can give to each person his right reward, according to his deeds—how he has lived" (TLB).

As you'll notice, it doesn't say that some people's hearts are more wicked than others. All of us have the potential for actions that can destroy others and ourselves.

Thankfully, God has chosen not to leave us this way. We would all be without hope if it weren't for God's grace. God says in Isaiah 43:25, "I, yes, I alone am he who blots away your sins for my own sake and will never think of them again" (TLB).

Whatever you have done, God isn't surprised. He not only forgives you, but also will pursue you the rest of your life to somehow demonstrate his unconditional forgiveness.

Your own recognition of wrong is proof of that pursuit. God has opened up your heart so you can take a look at its ugliness. Now you must make a decision whether you want to leave it that way or allow him to come in and clean it up.

"Come, let's talk this over!" says the Lord; "no matter how deep the stain of your sins, I can take it out and make you as clean as freshly fallen snow. Even if you are stained as red as crimson, I can make you white as wool!" (Isaiah 1:18, TLB).

Because God offers forgiveness, even to the most wicked person, he demonstrates his true nature. Without his forgiveness, everyone would have no hope whatsoever. The question is not, "How can God forgive you?" The question is, "God loves you so much, how can he not forgive you?"

It seems like every other month my dad is complaining about seeing another TV preacher getting into trouble or a local pastor who molested someone. What do I say to people who point to the hypocrites in this world as their reason for giving God the cold shoulder?

ISAIAH 29:13–14

The Lord says: "These people come near to me with their mouth and honor me with their lips, but their hearts are far from me. Their worship of me is made up only of rules taught by men. Therefore once more I will astound these people with wonder upon wonder; the wisdom of the wise will perish, the intelligence of the intelligent will vanish."

Unfortunately, even some of God's own kids can act shamefully. In fact, there is not a Christian alive who, at one time or another, hasn't betrayed God by his or her actions.

The word *hypocrisy* means claiming to be a certain type of person while acting like someone else. Unfortunately, people often reject a relationship with God because his children don't act like they know him. That's one reason why God is so hacked off at hypocrites who claim to be followers but really aren't.

Jesus said, "More than anything else, beware of these Pharisees and the way they pretend to be good when they aren't. But such hypocrisy cannot be hidden forever. It will become as evident as yeast in dough. Whatever they have said in the dark shall be heard in the light, and what you have whispered in the inner rooms shall be broadcast from the housetops for all to hear!" (Luke 12:1–3, TLB).

When the final act draws to a close, some of the first to receive God's wrath will be those who have been "play acting" with God. He is not impressed; they will be judged. "For we must all stand before Christ to be judged and have our lives laid bare—before him. Each of us will receive whatever he deserves for the good or bad things he has done in his earthly body" (2 Corinthians 5:10, TLB).

There is literally nothing you can do to prevent strangers from misrepresenting Christ. The only person you can prevent from being a hypocrite is *you*. Here are some ways to keep from becoming a hypocrite:

First, watch your own actions closely. Though *God* reads your heart, other people see your actions first. "Check up on yourselves. Are you really Christians? Do you pass the test? Do you feel Christ's presence and power more and more within you? Or are you just pretending to be Christians when actually you aren't at all?" (2 Corinthians 13:5, TLB). If what you do doesn't match what you tell others you believe, get ready to be called a hypocrite.

Second, don't come down too hard on other people. Remember that the only difference between you and those who aren't Christians is that you have received the *gift* of forgiveness.

Third, be quick to admit when you make a mistake. True humility is rare in our culture, but for some reason people are drawn to those who can readily admit their mistakes. It's called being genuine.

CHAPTER 56

I used to like to go to parties a lot before I became a Christian. Are parties bad?

MARK 2:13-17

*Once again Jesus went out beside the lake. A large crowd
came to him, and he began to teach them. As he walked along, he saw
Levi son of Alphaeus sitting at the tax collector's booth. "Follow me,"
Jesus told him, and Levi got up and followed him.*

*While Jesus was having dinner at Levi's house, many tax
collectors and "sinners" were eating with him and his disciples, for
there were many who followed him. When the teachers of the law who
were Pharisees saw him eating with the "sinners" and tax collectors,
they asked his disciples: "Why does he eat with tax collectors and
'sinners'?"*

*On hearing this, Jesus said to them, "It is not the healthy
who need a doctor, but the sick. I have not come to call the righteous,
but sinners."*

In answering this type of question, it's tough not to
sound heavy-handed. After all, teenage parties do not exactly have a great reputation. The key word to remember is
not yes or no, but *why*. Your motive is the key.

The motive behind going to parties is what God is most
concerned about. If it were to get drunk, take drugs, hit on
the opposite sex, then God wouldn't want you at parties.

And if there are illegal substances at the party, you shouldn't be there at all! God says, "Woe to those who are 'heroes' when it comes to drinking, and boast about the liquor they can hold" (Isaiah 5:22, TLB).

The motive might be to be seen with the "cool" people. Being seen at a party has a tendency to make someone feel accepted because they were in the same place as a popular person outside of school. But God accepts you as you are, and his acceptance is more important than anyone else's is.

If you've read the Gospel accounts on the life of Jesus, you can readily see that Jesus went to parties. But his motives were entirely different from the selfish ones described above. He went to shed light in the midst of darkness. He went to show people that he accepted them, and to communicate truth about the character of God.

Should you do the same? Perhaps, but here are a few questions you need to consider:

- What do your youth leader or parents think about your attending that party? Would you have to *not tell them* in order to go?
- Have you grown sufficiently in your faith that you'll not be tempted if there's pressure to drink (or whatever)?
- Do you know someone who will go with so you can encourage each other to stay clean?
- Are you going as a light or a hammer? That is, do you genuinely want to help those in darkness or do you want to pound on others to justify your own moral lifestyle?
- Is there a chance that you could be found "guilty by association"? When others hear you were at the party, how will they know you didn't drink? Is it worth the hassle it may cause in making sure your reputation stays intact?

Remember, although motive is the key, even the results of good motives may be more than you need to handle.

I hear a lot about the New Age movement. Some of my friends say they are into it now. How is this different from what I believe as a Christian?

1 CORINTHIANS 1:18–19

For the message of the cross is foolishness to those who are perishing, but to us who are being saved it is the power of God. For it is written: "I will destroy the wisdom of the wise; the intelligence of the intelligent I will frustrate."

The most convenient religion is one you create yourself. That, in essence, is what the New Age movement does for people. It allows them to create whatever rules they want to have about God, their behavior, and how to make it to the next life.

Generally, they believe that God is everywhere and in everybody. Because we are humans, we all have a unity of spirit that allows us to be brothers no matter what. God is not good or bad. In fact, each person is a god. He or she is the center of the universe. Morality, therefore, isn't important (since God is not seen as either good or bad). But the mind and intellect are very important because, supposedly, a person has to think deep thoughts to understand these concepts.

They believe that salvation comes through reincarnation. This means coming back to life again in the form of someone else, again and again, until you get it right. (Reincarnation is a lie; the Bible is very clear on this point. See Hebrews 9:27.)

There are so many strains within the New Age movement that it's impossible to outline them all. But the key for this type of thinking is the belief that there is no personal God, that human beings are not sinful, and that the next life is assured in some form, no matter what you have done here on earth. This is a very convenient religion if you just want to do your own thing.

But listen to God: "The Lord says: Cursed is the man who puts his trust in mortal man and turns his heart away from God" (Jeremiah 17:5, TLB). When people set their own beliefs and thoughts up as more important than what God thinks, they are actually being cursed by him!

Temptation to "think yourself" out of a relationship with God is everywhere. Nearly every belief within the New Age movement allows you to become your own god. Satan told Eve that she would become like God if she ate of the fruit of the tree (Genesis 3:1–6). People are being told they can be god of their life if they will just look away from the one, true God.

The Bible must be our authority on what we are to believe about God and what it takes to be saved from our sin. If it isn't, everyone can create their own religion to suit their own desires.

I'm afraid to give my whole life to God. I'm

thinking he's going to ask me to do things later

on, like be a missionary in another country. I

really don't want to do that. What happens if I

hold part of my life back from God?

JEREMIAH 29:11-13

"For I know the plans I have for you," declares the Lord,
"plans to prosper you and not to harm you, plans to give you hope
and a future. Then you will call upon me and come and pray to me,
and I will listen to you. You will seek me and find me when you seek
me with all your heart."

Imagine going out for basketball and telling the coach that you only wanted to practice and not play in the Friday night games. Or that you only wanted to play the first half of each game. How would your coach react? What would your teammates say?

Undoubtedly they would be a little miffed at your selfish attitude. After all, if you're going to be on the team, you should play in the game. And if you play, you shouldn't avoid the last half when your team might need you the most. Besides, playing the game is a lot better than practice. And the second half is when the game is on the line.

Unfortunately, many Christians by their attitudes and

their actions are telling the coach (God) two things: They don't really want the benefits and the fun of playing on the team (besides heaven, of course); and they don't want to contribute during the times when other people might need them the most.

God wants your whole life so he can make something extraordinary out of it. Jesus told his followers, "The thief's purpose is to steal, kill and destroy. My purpose is to give life in all its fullness" (John 10:10, TLB). That's a level of trust you haven't caught on to yet.

The Christian life was *never* meant to be done halfway. Some would say you couldn't do it halfway at all. You're either sold out to God or sold out to the world.

For God to give you "life in all its fullness," you must give your full life to God. Jesus said, "If you cling to your life, you will lose it; but if you give it up for me, you will save it" (Matthew 10:39, TLB).

If God asks you to be a missionary to another country, in effect he is saying, "I know you better than anyone else does. I made you and I love you more than you'll ever know. Because I put you together, I know what it will take to make you the happiest and most fulfilled in life. If you choose any other direction, you'll be settling for second best. Please don't."

God's goal isn't to make his kids miserable. He wants to lead us in a direction that will cause us to say, "The game wasn't easy, God, especially the last quarter. Thanks for believing in me enough to put me in. That was the best game ever."

Even though I know I'm going to heaven, I'm still afraid of dying. How can I quit being so afraid of death?

1 THESSALONIANS 4:13-14

Brothers, we do not want you to be ignorant about those who fall asleep, or to grieve like the rest of men, who have no hope. We believe that Jesus died and rose again and so we believe that God will bring with Jesus those who have fallen asleep in him.

Extreme fear of the unknown can cripple a person. Unfortunately, death is an unknown for many, even for Christians.

What will we find on the other side? How is God going to take me? Will heaven be an exciting place or will I get bored sitting on clouds and playing the harp? Will the people left behind be able to adjust? What if I die before I have a chance to get married or see some places I want to see?

Someone once said that trying to describe God and heaven to another person is like a dog telling another dog what it's like to be a human. It's impossible!

But death is not something that Christians have to fear. "Since we, God's children, are human beings—made of flesh and blood—he became flesh and blood too by being born in human form; for only as a human being could he die and in dying break the power of the devil who had the power of death. Only in that way could he deliver those who through fear of death have been living all their lives as slaves to constant dread" (Hebrews 2:14–15, TLB).

Death, especially for the Christian, isn't the end of the story. It's the gateway to a place of indescribable joy and beauty. It's the beginning of a new life!

Fear is a learned emotion. Through the years we're conditioned to fear certain things. Little kids aren't afraid of death because they don't understand it. Yet as they grow and see the responses of adults and the media to death, they learn that it's something awful to be avoided at all costs.

After we become Christians, we often need to go through a relearning process about death. Paul, the author of half the New Testament, said this about death: "For to me, living means opportunities to win people to Christ, and dying—well, that's better yet!" (Philippians 1:21, TLB).

Paul had learned that death would actually put an end to the struggles he faced on earth. He looked forward to the day when he could see Christ face-to-face. In the meantime, though, he had work to do—to win people to Christ. Life wasn't a chore, it was a privilege. He was able to help others lose their fear of death and show them how Jesus could take away the penalty of death.

Fear of dying doesn't disappear instantly. But as you spend time in the Bible and with other Christians who have the same hope as you do, you'll grow to realize that death is only a door to an eternity far better than your wildest dreams.

Who wrote the Bible, and how do I know if it really came from God?

2 TIMOTHY 3:16-17

*All Scripture is God-breathed and is useful for teaching,
rebuking, correcting and training in righteousness, so that the man of
God may be thoroughly equipped for every good work.*

God is the author of the Bible, but he worked through the minds of his chosen writers so they only wrote down what God wanted.

The Bible contains sixty-six books, written by about forty authors at various points in history. Many of the "books" are actually letters.

If you know a mathematician, ask him the probability of sixty-six separate documents, written over a period of fifteen hundred years, by forty different authors, not having any contradictions. He'd have to conclude what you've described is mathematically impossible. Yet that's exactly what God has done as he has arranged the Bible.

The theme, the history, the way the Bible reveals God's character, and especially the way it describes God's way of bringing salvation to men, are consistent throughout.

More important than how we got the Bible is why. God gave the Bible to us, as the passage above says, to prepare us for anything in order that we might do good to everyone.

God's Word serves as our offensive weapon against all of the problems we encounter. "For whatever God says to us is full of living power: it is sharper than the sharpest dagger, cutting swift and deep into our innermost thoughts and desires with all their parts, exposing us for what we really are" (Hebrews 4:12, TLB).

Facing problems in the right way is more important to God than preventing us from going through them. He's given us his Word to point to the solutions we need.

God is in the business of molding our character and strengthening us for future use. In the Bible he's given us all of the resources for strength we'll ever need.

Why are there so many rules to obey after you become a Christian?

MARK 12:28–31

One of the teachers of the law came and heard them debating. Noticing that Jesus had given them a good answer, he asked him, "Of all the commandments, which is the most important?"

"The most important one," answered Jesus, "is this: 'Hear, O Israel, the Lord our God, the Lord is one. Love the Lord your God with all your heart and with all your soul and with all your mind and with all your strength.' The second is this: 'Love your neighbor as yourself.' There is no commandment greater than these."

If you want to survive being lost in the wilderness for more than a night, there are certain things you must *have*, as well as *do*, in order to make it out safely. The basics you need are a knife, warm clothes, and some matches. These would help you find food, stay warm, make a shelter, and start a fire. Basic survival is the first order of business when you're lost.

The one instrument that's key for providing direction out of the wilderness is a compass. Without it, most could only guess which direction they should go. Pursuing a wrong course could delay finding safety. Your life might be in danger.

Survival as a Christian, especially in today's world, also depends on things that will not only provide basic survival, but will give the direction needed for future "safety."

The elements of survival, "the rules" you talked about, can vary, depending on what type of Christian group you're a part of. Most groups would use Scripture to back up what they believe are basic survival ingredients.

Examples of issues that are most disagreed upon within the Christian world include these: how much exposure to the secular media we should have (music, movies, TV); whether the opposite sexes should have physical contact while dating (hugging, kissing); when people reach twenty-one, whether they should drink any form of alcohol, even if they don't intend to get drunk.

The groups who would say "no" to all of the above have likely learned, through tough experiences, that involvement in these areas can lead to actions that would be extremely harmful to a growing Christian. Scripturally, there is a strong case to be made for this type of conclusion.

What needs to be considered above human opinions is, "What does God really expect of me?"

When Jesus was confronted with a similar question, his response was simple. He said to "love [God] with all your heart and soul and mind and strength" and to "love others as much as yourself. No other commandments are greater than these" (Mark 12:30–31, TLB).

To love God means to obey him (John 14:15). *Obedience* is a word that we don't normally like to talk about. We like to do our own thing. Yet it's the key to showing God we are really serious about following him. Loving God means not just allowing him into our lives but finding out what his heart is on the issues that can trip us up.

Loving others as much as ourselves also takes a lot of work. Most psychologists agree that ninety percent of the people spend ninety percent of their time thinking how they can get their own needs met! We are a very selfish people.

These two commandments by Jesus serve as a compass to our lives. Without them, we would wander in the wrong direction and would never really understand what it means to be a Christian.

The rest of the "rules" that we can get tired of hearing about are survival skills. They are not the end in themselves. They only push us closer to the goal of loving God (by obeying him) and loving others like we love ourselves.

People around me don't act like they need God. How can I share my faith in Christ with them if they don't feel a need to even talk about him, let alone get to know him?

HOSEA 13:6

*When I fed them, they were satisfied; when they were
satisfied, they became proud; then they forgot me.*

Rarely will people want a relationship with someone if they feel like they don't need him or her. The Bible is filled with stories of people who have actively rejected God because they felt no need—their lives were going too well. You probably know many people like this.

Still, when things are rough, people quickly pin the blame on God. This makes as much sense as a six-year-old hitting himself on the thumb with a hammer, and then blaming his dad.

"I saw you use your hammer once, Dad. And even though you told me not to use it, I chose to anyway. It's your job to make sure I never hurt myself with it. If I do hurt myself, it'll be your fault!"

People do the same with God.

"I'm going to take my life and run it the way I want to, God. But if things go wrong, it's your fault!"

Though you can't create within someone a need for God, here are some things you can do:

145

- Pray for your friends to be faced with a situation where they would have to look to God for help. The Prodigal Son had to feed pigs before he finally came to his senses and returned to the love of his father (see Luke 15:11–32). If your friends really want to go their own way, there is usually nothing you can do besides pray for them.
- Be ready to help them when they do have a need. Keep the friendship bridges built strong enough so your friends will come to you for help. Then you can point them to Christ. Seek the help of a mature Christian friend for advice on how to do this best.
- Look for people who are already hurt and share the Good News with them. With the number of problems in the world today, people are ready to hear some good news!
- Watch out for your own heart. The Bible is clear that certain things can cause us to take our eyes off of God. "Trust in your money and down you go! Trust in God and flourish as a tree!" (Proverbs 11:28, TLB). "Before every man there lies a wide and pleasant road that seems right but ends in death" (Proverbs 14:12).

The "easy" life of living separated from God is exactly how Satan wants us to live. The stakes are high. Being separated from God in this life affects our eternity.

CHAPTER 63

I've been a Christian about nine months. Although I've made a lot of friends who are Christians, I still have quite a few friends who aren't. Should I still be hanging out with those friends who aren't Christians?

2 CORINTHIANS 6:14–15

Do not be yoked together with unbelievers. For what do righteousness and wickedness have in common? Or what fellowship can light have with darkness? What harmony is there between Christ and Belial? What does a believer have in common with an unbeliever?

Find a quarter and two pennies. Place the quarter on a table. Put the two pennies about five inches below the quarter, one inch apart.

Now, pretend God is the quarter, you are the penny on the left, and your friend or girl/boyfriend is on the right. As you grow closer to God, move your penny up an inch or two. What happens to the distance between you and your friend? It gets wider! When only one person in a friendship moves closer to God, that's what happens to the relationship automatically!

There are degrees in friendships and stages we go through to make them stronger. Just like in a guy/girl relationship, you progress from one stage (degree) to another. The common denominator is time.

Think about the friends you used to hang around with. You probably did the same things, used the same slang, laughed at the same type of jokes, etc. For someone who wants to grow spiritually, hanging around with old friends who aren't Christians will likely not get you to the goal of becoming a stronger Christian. That's what this verse is about. If you spend all of your deeper friendship time with unbelievers, it's like trying to mix light and dark. Though light can shine in the dark, darkness can make that light look very dim.

God doesn't want you to be totally isolated from those who aren't Christians. In fact, if you get to the point where you don't have any non-Christian friends, you're probably doing something wrong. If we're going to be Christ's representative to those who don't know him (see 2 Corinthians 5:18–20), we have to be around them!

But if a friendship or a dating relationship with someone who isn't a Christian causes your faith to go downhill, you probably should keep your distance from them. You need to be around people who will be your friend *and* help you grow spiritually at the same time. "Be with wise men and become wise. Be with evil men and become evil" (Proverbs 13:20, TLB).

Because of my shyness and my family situation, I find it tough to let people get close to me. As a Christian, I hear all of the time how much God loves me. How close does God want to get with me?

REVELATION 2:4

Yet I hold this against you: You have forsaken your first love.

As close as you'll let him.

It's hard to imagine that God knows everything about us yet still wants to be a Father to us. King David, the author of most of the Psalms, knew how close God wants to be. He says, "How precious it is, Lord, to realize that you are thinking about me constantly! I can't even count how many times a day your thoughts turn toward me. And when I waken in the morning, you are still thinking of me!" (Psalm 139:17–18, TLB).

Knowing how much God thinks about us should give us an incredible feeling of worth. Our response to God's constant attentiveness, however, should never be out of obligation. God would absolutely hate it if we chose to love him only because we felt we had to.

For some, because of a bad family history or a shy, withdrawn personality, that statement will mean different things. It's tough to learn to love someone like God when we have never seen a good example before.

This verse in Revelation warns us not to allow our love for God to grow weaker. God wants us to progress and grow beyond our initial commitment to him, just like in a marriage, where love should continue to grow. Unfortunately, this doesn't always happen. Many people who become Christians are really excited about their new relationship with God. But as problems come up, the excitement often wears off (just like what happens in some marriages).

To maintain a growing relationship with God, the key word is *time*: time daily with him, time with others who know him, and time (in years) to grow to appreciate his love for you.

Though God is eager for an intimate relationship with us, he'll wait for the day when we'll experience for ourselves what loving him really means.

CHAPTER 65

My mom used to go to church, but she doesn't anymore. What can I do to get her to give God more attention?

JEREMIAH 2:13

My people have committed two sins: They have forsaken me, the spring of living water, and have dug their own cisterns, broken cisterns that cannot hold water.

Going from a close relationship with Christ to total neglect is like going from a two-wheeled bike to one with training wheels. It seems safer, but it's not half the fun.

Unfortunately, you'll see many people start out strong in their walk with God, but for some reason they'll fade and eventually drop off. Remember that the Christian life is not a hundred-yard dash, it's a long-distance race, a *marathon*! How you start is not nearly as important as how you finish.

In a long race, many people get weary of waiting for the prize and decide to quit. Your mother sounds like an example of that type. To survive as a person, she has found other things that have temporarily given her the idea everything is okay.

As this verse says, when people reject God they need other things to hold life together. For everyone who turns away from God, those other things are but "broken water pots" that don't hold anything of value.

And like the person who goes back to the bike with training wheels because it's safer, some people allow distractions to push God aside because they're running after the wrong prize.

If people believe that the Christian life means having their problems solved immediately, always being treated right by people, never having doubts about the future, having prayers always answered within a week, and always being entertained in church, then people *are* running after the wrong prize! They'll be disappointed, grow tired, and give up.

But if our goal is simply getting to know the God who created us and loved us enough to die on a cross to save us from our sin, then we'll never grow weary. There's always something new to discover about the richness and depth of God's love for us.

Don't try to change your mom. She'll likely not appreciate it, no matter how good your motives are. Instead, give God permission to change you! Focus on how well you are doing.

"Beware then of your own hearts, dear brothers, lest you find that they, too, are evil and unbelieving and are leading you away from the living God. . . . For if we are faithful to the end, trusting God just as we did when we first became Christians, we will share in all that belongs to Christ" (Hebrews 3:12, 14, TLB).

Become more diligent in doing your chores and homework. Begin to treat your brothers and sisters better than you have. Pray that your mom will see these changes and will ask you about it. Continually pray for her. Then give God time to work. Remember that he wants her back in a right relationship with him more than you do.

CHAPTER 66

Before I became a Christian, I put my mind through some stuff that was real garbage. How do I clean up my thought life?

PHILIPPIANS 4:8

Finally, brothers, whatever is true, whatever is noble, whatever is right, whatever is pure, whatever is lovely, whatever is admirable—if anything is excellent or praiseworthy—think about such things.

Almost every school in America is equipped with computers. Most businesses remain competitive because they're able to access and store large amounts of information. Computers are serving nearly every segment of society. But they have one flaw—they are dependent on the programs and information put into them.

Your mind works a lot like a computer. If it's programmed to think about crud, that's what will happen. If it's programmed to think about things that are healthy, you'll think healthy thoughts. It's really very simple.

The hard part comes in trying to keep out the unhealthy thoughts. Often, it only takes a few exposures to an image that's against God's goodness to cause you to forget the good and pursue the bad. Just think what happens when we are repeatedly exposed to images that pollute! You don't have to be a rocket scientist to realize our world is succeeding in polluting a lot of minds.

So what's God's solution? Reprogram the mind! For this job, there are no shortcuts. The more exposure to things that have polluted us—whether from movies, magazines, TV, music, concerts*, or just the everyday conversation with friends who don't care what they say—the longer it will take to clear the mind of destructive thought patterns.

The reprogramming process begins when we realize that destructive thoughts and images are trying to get a foothold in our mind, and we start to kick them out. "And we take captive every thought to make it obedient to Christ" (2 Corinthians 10:5).

The next step is choosing to dwell on what is positive and good. Paul says, "Let heaven fill your thoughts; don't spend your time worrying about things down here" (Colossians 3:2, TLB).

Finally, we need to renew our minds. "Don't copy the behavior and customs of this world, but be a new and different person with a fresh newness in all you do and think. Then you will learn from your own experience how his ways will really satisfy you" (Romans 12:2, TLB).

Satan has lost the battle when it comes to our eternal destiny. His alternate plan is to keep our mind focused away from the goodness of God. He now wants to wage war in our minds so that the Christian life seems too hard to maintain. If he can discourage us, he may get us to throw in the towel and admit defeat.

The battle now is being waged in the thought life. Call upon God to rescue you from destructive thoughts, and he will do it!

---

*There is nothing inherently evil about these forms of communication—unless they send an unhealthy message that is contrary to what God says.

What does it mean to grow as a Christian?

EPHESIANS 4:14–15

*Then we will no longer be infants, tossed back and forth by
the waves, and blown here and there by every wind of teaching and
by the cunning and craftiness of men in their deceitful scheming.
Instead, speaking the truth in love, we will in all things grow up into
him who is the Head, that is, Christ.*

Spiritual growth is a lot like physical growth. In order to
stay healthy and grow physically, we must eat the right
foods, exercise, and get plenty of rest. You've heard this message since you were a child. To grow spiritually involves the
same formula.

Eating the right foods as a Christian means consuming the
right spiritual "food." Many Christians are trying to survive
on "fast food" to have a strong faith. That is, they watch
Christian TV, read Christian magazines, and listen to Christian music, but they rarely pay attention to God's Word.

There's only one food that will nourish our souls—the
Bible. Everything else is only meant to be like "vitamin sup-
plements." Imagine if all we ate were vitamins. Yes, we'd
have the right nutrients, but we wouldn't have the substance
needed for muscle, bone, and cell development.

Exercise as a Christian involves resisting temptations, en-
during trials, serving others, and telling others about our
faith.

If all we did was eat pop, candy, pizza, or steak and baked
potatoes, and never worked off the carbohydrates and cal-

ories, we'd get fat! Our bodies were meant to be physically pushed in order to stay strong. This is the reason behind the trials we face every day. "These trials are only to test your faith, to see whether or not it is strong and pure. It is being tested as fire tests gold; so if your faith remains strong after being tried in the test tube of fiery trials, it will bring you much praise and glory and honor on the day of his return" (1 Peter 1:7, TLB).

Rest for the Christian is worship. Our world has a tendency to tighten us up, like a rubber band pulled to the limit. Unless we take time weekly (and daily!) to recognize and worship God, he doesn't have the opportunity to minister to our needs. We need sleep, rest, and times of vacation in order to get our physical batteries recharged. And our spirits need worship and renewal to keep our *spiritual* batteries recharged, as well.

Growth takes time—a lifetime! The most important aspect of growth is to daily realize we are growing in a relationship, not just right behavior. Trying to "be good" all of the time can be discouraging. All of us fail. That's why we must realize the Christian life is learning how to love the person of Jesus Christ more each day. "You love him even though you have never seen him; though not seeing him, you trust him; and even now you are happy with inexpressible joy that comes from heaven itself. And your further reward for trusting him will be the salvation of your souls" (1 Peter 1:8–9, TLB).

My older brother is always making fun of my new faith. How do I get him to stop?

LUKE 12:51–53

"Do you think I came to bring peace on earth? No, I tell you, but division. From now on there will be five in one family divided against each other, three against two and two against three. They will be divided, father against son and son against father, mother against daughter and daughter against mother, mother-in-law against daughter-in-law and daughter-in-law against mother-in-law."

People ridicule what they don't understand or what they wish they had themselves. It's really tough, though, when it comes from someone in your own family!

Your best defense is a quiet offense. "Don't snap back at those who say unkind things about you. Instead, pray for God's help for them, for we are to be kind to others, and God will bless us for it" (1 Peter 3:9, TLB).

When anyone makes fun of your faith, hold your tongue, pray for the person, be kind to him or her, and then wait for God's blessing. This verse ends with a promise directly from God. Though it doesn't say *when* God will bless you or *how* God will bless you, it promises that he *will* bless you.

Here are some steps to take when facing opposition for your faith (see 1 Peter 3:13–15):

First, check your attitude. If you understand that God is allowing you to experience this for a reason, you'll be able to thank him for it. It means he believes in you enough to allow you to be tested.

Second, quietly trust yourself to Christ. Since you've made the step to trust Christ to be Lord of your life, allow him to be Lord over the results of your circumstances. God is trying to build within you endurance in order to develop your character.

Third, be real and be ready to explain your faith as best you can when the opportunities arise. By helping your brother better understand you're the same person (faults and all), he'll likely not verbally rank on you as often. Because the outward behavior of Christians gets better after the inward change has occurred, he may be threatened by your good life. You become a higher standard to measure up to around the house.

Admitting your faults while trying not to be "holier than thou" may disarm your brother to the point that he'll see you're not a threat. Talk it over with him as "adult" as you can.

Even doing all of this still may not relieve the tension. So, "Remember, if God wants you to suffer, it is better to suffer for doing good than for doing wrong!" (1 Peter 3:17, TLB).

It's hard to believe in anything you can't see. Why has God made it so tough on people who would believe in him if only they could see him?

1 PETER 1:8-9

Though you have not seen him, you love him; and even though you do not see him now, you believe in him and are filled with an inexpressible and glorious joy, for you are receiving the goal of your faith, the salvation of your souls.

God is big, strong, powerful, and fully able to appear to anyone he wants. But if he did that, most people would feel forced or intimidated into following his orders rather than loved into following his example. God wants us to respond out of love for him—not fear!

The truth is that people *can* see God—through the eyes of faith. This means taking God at his Word—opening ourselves up to him. Some people say seeing is believing. The truth is, believing is seeing. "You can never please God without faith, without depending on him. Anyone who wants to come to God must believe that there is a God and that he rewards those who sincerely look for him" (Hebrews 11:6, TLB).

Trying to find a standard by which everyone in the world could enter into his presence was no easy task. Consider the alternatives, many of which are currently being used by the cults:

Do enough good works to get to heaven. If this were God's standard, what would happen to those who, at the end of their lives, realized their need for God? Do they get shut out because it took them longer to catch on? Then someone would have to decide how many good works—and what kind—would have to be done in order to go to heaven. Who makes this decision?

Go to church every week. Again, we have the problem of those who decide too late. Also, which church do you call the right one? How can everyone in the world go to a specific type of church?

Give enough money to the church and/or the poor. What happens if you're poor?

These and other man-made ideas about how to please God will not work—only faith ensures that everyone will have a chance. God, in his wisdom, knew that. He had to be fair.

All of us believe in things we have never seen. A person in history. Gravity. The wind. *Everyone* has the capacity to believe things that aren't seen. The bottom line for most who say, "I can't believe in something I haven't seen," is "I won't believe in God because I want to run my own life." God doesn't work that way. Each person must trust in Christ, acknowledging him as Savior.

God has not promised to show us the road ahead. He has only promised to walk with us as we go. Faith is a daily choice to believe in God's love, his promises, his presence, and his provision for our needs. We want peace, direction, purpose, and love—God wants to give this and more to those who have faith.

"Blessed are those who haven't seen me and believe anyway" (John 20:29, TLB).

Trying to stay pure and not sin seems like a full-time job. How can anyone stay pure? Why would anyone want to?

1 TIMOTHY 6:11–12

But you, man of God, flee from all this, and pursue righteousness, godliness, faith, love, endurance and gentleness. Fight the good fight of the faith. Take hold of the eternal life to which you were called when you made your good confession in the presence of many witnesses.

Jesus talked a lot about the Pharisees. These men had taken the Old Testament law and added even more details. They created long lists of do's and don'ts about behavior of every kind. They wanted to be pure! Many of them *were* very, very good.

But in Matthew 5:20, Jesus made an incredible statement! "But I warn you—unless your goodness is greater than that of the Pharisees and other Jewish leaders, you can't get into the Kingdom of Heaven at all!" (TLB)

Wow! If the Pharisees couldn't make it, then who can?

Those who make it into the kingdom of heaven are not just pure on the outside, like the Pharisees. Everyone can make sure their behavior is correct (at least for a while).

What Jesus was talking about is being pure on the inside. For Christians, purity only comes through accepting Christ's death on the cross as our punishment for our sins. When we do this, we take on Christ's goodness, and in God's eyes, we are pure and worthy of eternity in heaven! Now, that's a pretty good deal!

But it doesn't stop there. God wants us to be like Jesus. This is a lifetime process of allowing God to mold us and change us. It's what keeps the Christian life fun, interesting, and challenging.

He wants us to be pure so that he can better use us to help others. Staying pure, from the inside, allows the lines of communication and blessing to flow between God and us; we become a lump of clay, ready to be molded into something useful.

Jesus called the Pharisees "whitewashed tombs . . . full of dead men's bones" (Matthew 23:27). That is, they looked okay from the outside, but there was nothing living on the inside. Their motives for right living were only so people would be impressed by their "goodness."

Christians who are really alive realize their eternity is settled. But they also genuinely want to be more like the one who paid such a high price for their souls—Jesus. Their motivation is not to parade their goodness in front of others, but rather to please God.

Staying pure and growing as a Christian *are* full-time jobs. But the wages are incredible! The reward of seeing your life count by helping others brings more pleasure than any amount of money ever could.

CHAPTER 71

My friends are always doing things that my conscience won't let me get away with, yet they never seem to get caught. Why does it seem like a lot of bad stuff never gets punished?

AMOS 6:6–7

You drink wine by the bowlful and use the finest lotions, but you do not grieve over the ruin of Joseph. Therefore you will be among the first to go into exile; your feasting and lounging will end.

At the dentist, novocain deadens the nerves in our mouth so we won't feel the pain of the drill. The conscience can also be numbed by repeated sin, so that the person no longer feels guilty about wrong behavior. Be glad that you have an active conscience. It means that you're still sensitive to sin.

In response to your question, all sins have consequences. Some wrong actions have immediate consequences. If someone is cheating on a test while the teacher is watching, the immediate consequence will be an F.

Other actions have short-term, delayed consequences. Some people choose to cheat on their income tax returns. They may get away with it for a year or two, but eventually, the IRS audits their returns, discovers the problems, and then levies a hefty fine or even sends them to prison.

Still other actions never seem to get punished. The key

word is *seem*. The Bible is very clear about what will happen in the long run to actions contrary to God's plan.

"Don't be misled; remember that you can't ignore God and get away with it: a man will always reap just the kind of crop he sows! If he sows to please his own wrong desires, he will be planting seeds of evil and he will surely reap a harvest of spiritual decay and death; but if he plants the good things of the Spirit, he will reap the everlasting life which the Holy Spirit gives him" (Galatians 6:7–8, TLB).

If we sow bad actions, we'll reap the fruit of that kind of seed. The same is true when we sow things that are good. If we are genuinely trying to follow close to God, reading our Bible, communicating with him, etc., God will use us, and we'll reap a wonderful harvest.

It can get tiring, however, always trying to be good, especially when there's so much bad all around us. That's when we have to remember God's promise of the eventual harvest. "And let us not get tired of doing what is right, for after a while we will reap a harvest of blessing if we don't get discouraged and give up" (Galatians 6:9, TLB).

The prophet Amos told the people of Israel what would happen if they didn't shape up. They were numb toward the things of God. His predictions didn't immediately come true. After many years, however, he proved to be right. The Israelites were conquered by the Assyrians and were made slaves, receiving exactly what they had given out.

It doesn't feel like I'm making too much progress as a Christian. It even seems like I'm going backward. What can I do to reverse my reversal?

EZEKIEL 14:1–5

Some of the elders of Israel came to me and sat down in front of me. Then the word of the Lord came to me: "Son of man, these men have set up idols in their hearts and put wicked stumbling blocks before their faces. Should I let them inquire of me at all? Therefore speak to them and tell them, 'This is what the Sovereign Lord says: When any Israelite sets up idols in his heart and puts a wicked stumbling block before his face and then goes to a prophet, I the Lord will answer him myself in keeping with his great idolatry. I will do this to recapture the hearts of the people of Israel, who have all deserted me for their idols.' "

Until about age twenty-five, we grow physically. After twenty-five, we start to die. Fortunately, it usually takes another fifty to seventy years before the dying process is complete!

Relationships can go through a living and dying process, too. Our relationship with God is either living and growing, or it's in the process of dying. There is no such thing as leveling out and staying even.

You've hit the first stage of beginning to spiritually grow again. You recognize that you've been dying.

The second stage is discovering what caused the dying process. God confronted his people continually about this issue. Speaking through Ezekiel, he pinpointed the problem as idols that had replaced God in their hearts. That is, they had placed their affections on other things instead of God.

What has been pushing God out of your life? Is it TV, a friendship, sports, a boyfriend or girlfriend, music, fun, apathy? Once you recognize what has caused your heart to be drawn away from God, the next step is absolutely necessary. Turn around! This means confessing the problem to God and turning it over to his control (see 1 John 1:9).

God has no desire to hold our neglect of him against us. He just wants us to admit we've gone astray and then get on with maintaining a steady growth with him.

The third step is one many Christians forget—finding someone who will encourage us, ask us the tough questions, kick us in the pants when we need it, and pray for us; someone who'll take the challenge of helping to guard our souls. The Bible calls this person a "shepherd."

This could be a friend your own age who has a real desire to grow spiritually. It could be a Christian adult whom you like and respect (teacher, youth pastor, or someone from your church). Anyone who'll genuinely be concerned for you and will always pull for you. It may seem someone like this is tough to find, but they're out there.

God knows you have a need to grow. He knows, too, that it's very difficult to grow by yourself. "Two can accomplish more than twice as much as one, for the results can be much better. If one falls, the other pulls him up; but if a man falls when he is alone, he's in trouble" (Ecclesiastes 4:9–10, TLB).

Ask God to send such a person into your life. This may seem scary at first, but Christians who are consistently growing in their faith have learned the secret of giving others permission to help them stay on track. As long as you live, seek out someone who will walk with you. It will keep you from falling and provide you with many close, lifelong friends.

I see the offering plate passed every week in church. I'm only a kid. Am I supposed to be giving my money to the church?

MALACHI 3:8–10

"Will a man rob God? Yet you rob me.

"But you ask, 'How do we rob you?'

"In tithes and offerings. You are under a curse—the whole nation of you—because you are robbing me. Bring the whole tithe into the storehouse, that there may be food in my house. Test me in this," says the Lord Almighty, *"and see if I will not throw open the floodgates of heaven and pour out so much blessing that you will not have room enough for it."*

Jesus talked about money and possessions more than he talked about anything else. That's because money, more than any other possession, can take a strong foothold in our life. It can even control us. Money by itself, of course, isn't evil. But the love of money leads to all sorts of problems (see 1 Timothy 6:10).

Though not loaded with money, young people almost always have cash to spend from odd jobs, gifts, and allowance.

If you were to track where your money goes, you're likely spending it on clothes, music, junk food, perhaps gas for the car (if you drive), and, once in a while, gifts for others. Most of your money you spend on *yourself*.

God doesn't want *anything* to take his place in your life. For many, money often becomes their god, especially for those who don't know Christ. Why is this so? "You cannot serve two masters: God and money. For you will hate one and love the other, or else the other way around"(Matthew 6:24, TLB).

The best way to keep from making money our god is to learn the joy of giving it away. And the younger you are when you start, the sooner you'll form the habit.

God doesn't need our money. He already owns everything! But *we* have a need to give it away. It's an incredible feeling to see our money go for something besides ourselves.

Here is a suggestion on how to start giving your money back to God. Each time you get some (whether through employment, allowance, or gift), take ten percent out and put it in an envelope that says "Jesus" on it. It doesn't matter if it's fifty cents from a five-dollar allowance or ten dollars from a hundred-dollar paycheck. Collect it for a month.

Next, decide where you want to give it away. Most churches have missionaries they support (people who are in the U.S. or overseas who have given their lives to spread the Good News of Jesus Christ). Select a missionary and ask to be put on their monthly prayer letter list. By giving to a missionary (even if it's $7.23 a month!), you're furthering the cause of Christ here on earth—and you're making wise investments in others' eternity! Remember, it doesn't matter how much you give, it only matters that you give what you can. See Luke 21:1–4 for a good illustration of this point.

Another suggestion is to support a child overseas who needs the basics to survive. There are several good organizations that will give you the name of a needy child you can help support, usually for about twenty dollars per month. This may be a larger investment than you want to make, but the fun of knowing you're helping a real person is worth it!

Of course, you can also give it directly to your church in

the offering plate and let them decide on how to use it, too.

Seeing your money go to something besides yourself may hurt a little at first. Eventually, however, you'll find you're having such a good time giving that you'll want to give more!

CHAPTER 74

I feel guilty more often now that I'm a Christian.

Sometimes the guilt comes on for just little stuff

that I used to never give a second thought about.

When do I need to ask God for forgiveness?

JAMES 4:17

Anyone, then, who knows the good he ought to do and doesn't
do it, sins.

God's goal is not to overwhelm us with our sin to the point that we become discouraged. He's wise enough to know when to prompt his Spirit to point out sin in our lives.

Some people come to faith in Christ and they are basically pretty good people. They don't have many destructive habits to overcome, and their parents have tried to teach them right from wrong.

Others come to Christ with a lot of sin baggage. Either no one tried to influence their value system or they deliberately avoided making right choices.

Although each person is unique, we're the same when it comes to our nature—we're sinners. We want to play God in our own lives. This is called "original sin." Though not a biblical term, it describes well the dilemma we were faced with before God sent Jesus to die in our place.

When we receive Christ as Savior, God declares us "not guilty." But this doesn't mean that we're perfect and don't sin anymore. We must daily deal with sin while we're still alive on earth. It's part of being human. Christians, like everyone, have two types of sin to deal with: past sins and present sins.

As I said, when we become Christians, all of our past sins are wiped away. "He has removed our sins as far away from us as the east is from the west" (Psalms 103:12, TLB). That's a distance that can't even be measured!

Ideally, having past sin taken away should take away the guilt feelings. We can put the past behind us. We're forgiven.

But what about present sin? One of the roles of the Holy Spirit is to remind us when we sin. He doesn't do this to condemn us, but to prompt us to confess our sin, forsake it, and move on. We confess to him to keep the communication channels with God open and to keep our relationship with him close. So we should talk to God about our life and confess our sin whenever we need to.

And remember, sin isn't limited to doing what is wrong. It also includes *not* doing what's right. The passage in James 4:17 is plain. "Remember, too, that knowing what is right to do and then not doing it is sin" (TLB).

If we know it's right to help a friend with homework . . . quench the gossip at the lunch table . . . give our folks the whole truth instead of only part of it . . . turn off the TV and spend time with God . . . and don't do it—we sin!

Let God do the convicting in your life, not others, and you'll be glad to confess your sins to him. He's eager to clear away the barriers between you and start fresh.

I've always been taught to be self-sufficient. My youth leader says this isn't right. What's wrong with being proud about doing your best?

LUKE 18:9-14

To some who were confident of their own righteousness and looked down on everybody else, Jesus told this parable: "Two men went up to the temple to pray, one a Pharisee and the other a tax collector. The Pharisee stood up and prayed about himself: 'God, I thank you that I am not like all other men—robbers, evildoers, adulterers—or even like this tax collector. I fast twice a week and give a tenth of all I get.'

"But the tax collector stood at a distance. He would not even look up to heaven, but beat his breast and said, 'God, have mercy on me, a sinner.'

"I tell you that this man, rather than the other, went home justified before God. For everyone who exalts himself will be humbled and he who humbles himself will be exalted."

Have you known kids who thought they were so good in sports that they rarely listened to the coach? Though all coaches love to have good talent, most would settle for team members with a few skills but who are *teachable*. An athlete is much easier to mold than to push.

Being totally self-reliant is sort of like the athletes who

allow the coach to give them advice *only when they want it*. Before long the athlete will start to deteriorate, in talent *and* in the eyes of the coach. In the same way, we need to depend on God to lead us.

God wants us always to try to do our best. We should never try to do anything halfway. But there's a difference between *our best* and allowing God to do *his best through us*.

Taking the credit for everything we do is called pride— it's a dangerous attitude.

There's a good type of pride that comes from doing a job well. Perhaps we've worked hard, persevered through some problems, and everything has come out great. We walk a fine line, though, when *we* are tempted to take the credit.

God wants us to recognize that he gave us our life and talents. When we do, it shows humility and a deep respect for him.

The Pharisee in Luke 18 is a perfect example of someone with a "bad pride." He was proud of his holy life. Although he acted like he was talking to God, he was really just talking to himself.

On the flip side is the tax collector. He had nothing to be proud of, especially in his relationship with God. In humility, he asked God for mercy.

If we go through life with an I-can-make-it-okay-by-myself attitude, we're really saying to God, "I don't really need you after all." Remember, "Pride goes before destruction and a haughty spirit before a fall" (Proverbs 16:18).

CHAPTER 76

I wish God would do more miracles in my life. I've heard people talk about what he's done for them—incredible stuff! Why don't amazing things happen more often?

JOEL 2:28–32

And afterward, I will pour out my Spirit on all people. Your sons and daughters will prophesy, your old men will dream dreams, your young men will see visions. Even on my servants, both men and women, I will pour out my Spirit in those days. I will show wonders in the heavens and on the earth, blood and fire and billows of smoke. The sun will be turned to darkness and the moon to blood before the coming of the great and dreadful day of the Lord. And everyone who calls on the name of the Lord will be saved; for on Mount Zion and in Jerusalem there will be deliverance, as the Lord has said, among the survivors whom the Lord calls.

Miracles are great to have, but the best miracle God could ever perform is the miracle of salvation.

That God has actually chosen to forgive us from our sin and come into our hearts and live inside us is an incredible miracle. We should thank him for that every day. But often we don't.

Some teachers of the law once came to Jesus and asked him to show them a miracle (Matthew 12:38). He answered that they wouldn't see any greater miracle than his being three days in the ground then coming back to life! But they weren't satisfied.

The real question is what kind of miracles you want God to do in your life.

Do you want him to give you *As* in subjects you haven't studied for? Allow you to score the winning touchdown so people will notice you? Perform some healing of an injury or sickness to "prove" he's still in your life? If so, you'll be disappointed.

But if you want to see him do miracles in the lives of those around you, stand back. That's the kind he specializes in. You'll find the most exciting miracles are when God uses you to lead someone else to him.

Small or large miracles God does in your life are great. And the longer you follow Christ, the more you'll see things happen. But when the eternal destiny of someone is changed, and God chooses to use you to have a part in it, the "high" you'll experience will be unlike any other. The goal is to be used by God. The feelings are just a bonus.

Don't get caught in the trap of wanting a Santa Claus-type of God who's always bringing you presents. Since this type of God doesn't exist, you'll end up being disappointed.

Instead, ask God to use you to perform the greatest miracle of all—seeing others humbly ask God to forgive their sin.

I want my Christian friends to grow in their faith as fast as I am. When I'm around them, it doesn't seem like they're acting much like believers. Why don't some people grow?

ACTS 18:24–26

Meanwhile a Jew named Apollos, a native of Alexandria, came to Ephesus. He was a learned man, with a thorough knowledge of the Scriptures. He had been instructed in the way of the Lord, and he spoke with great fervor and taught about Jesus accurately, though he knew only the baptism of John. He began to speak boldly in the synagogue. When Priscilla and Aquila heard him, they invited him to their home and explained to him the way of God more adequately.

It's *hugely* important to realize that all Christians grow on their own timetable, not someone else's. Just as people grow physically at different rates, most Christians don't hit their "growth spurt" at the same time. How fast Christians grow depends on a number of circumstances:

- The influence of their family is one of the biggest reasons why Christians grow at different rates. If Mom or Dad isn't growing, it's probably tougher for the son or daughter.
- The habits they had before they came to Christ will especially keep new believers from hitting the ground run-

ning. If they were media junkies who listened to hours of secular music, watched every R-rated movie that came out, compared themselves with all of the teen magazines, then they have some mind habits to retrain.

- How disciplined they are in reading their Bible, praying, and going to church will affect a Christian's rate of growth.
- Sometimes, like in the passage above, there's simply an information gap. Once Apollos learned a few more things about the faith, he was able to move to new levels of devotion and service.
- What type of friends Christians have will especially affect how quickly they grow.

I can tell you're concerned about your friends and wondering what you can do to help. The fruit of their lives is often the determiner in whether you should treat them like a non-Christian or a struggling believer. It doesn't sound like your friends are new Christians who are still unlearning old habits. More than likely, they need someone (like you) to gently point them in the right direction. How do you best do that?

The only thing you can do is to try to be as consistent as possible without being perfect. What I mean by that is that people, especially those of us who are aware of our sins and shortcomings, have a difficult time relating to someone who never makes mistakes (or is afraid to let others see them as mistake-prone believers). Most of us relate best to someone human. That's one reason why Jesus came to earth—to help us be able to relate to God. If God remained in heaven, then we'd always think he was too far away to touch.

Your sharing your weaknesses with others may give them the motivation to be real with you. Then, after they've shared something about themselves, perhaps they'll open the door so you can tell how Christ is working in your life. Usually, however, you have to wait until they give you permission to help. Unsolicited advice will usually make you look judgmental.

The relationship you have with your friends is the key. If you can treat them with grace—the way God treats us—they will one day have the courage to seek a closer walk with Christ.

Above all, keep praying for them. Wear God out with their name, and then look for him to be doing some changes. Satan, our enemy, is persistent. We must be, too.

I've been praying that my dad would become a Christian for more than six months. Why hasn't God answered my prayer?

MATTHEW 7:7–11

"Ask and it will be given to you; seek and you will find; knock and the door will be opened to you. For everyone who asks receives; he who seeks finds; and to him who knocks, the door will be opened.

"Which of you, if his son asks for bread, will give him a stone? Or if he asks for a fish, will give him a snake? If you, then, though you are evil, know how to give good gifts to your children, how much more will your Father in heaven give good gifts to those who ask him!"

God answers our prayers in three different ways: yes, no, and wait.

In our instant society, where everything happens when we want it, *wait* answers are not the ones we're accustomed to hearing. Especially when it seems as if the prayer is not being answered. But maybe it is.

God, in his perfect wisdom, knows the perfect way to lead people to a relationship with him. If we try to manipulate circumstances apart from God's will, these people may say no instead of yes.

Perhaps there's no one in your dad's life right now who would help him grow. God doesn't want new Christians to be left to fend for themselves. He knows that spiritual babies (no matter how old they are!) need attentive, spiritual care.

Maybe there are important questions still unanswered that would cause your dad to respond out of emotion rather than with his will. An emotional decision that has not counted the cost of following Christ won't last. There are simply too many pressures and pleasures available to distract a person from sticking to a commitment.

Perhaps there are hurts or misconceptions about God and the church that still need to be worked through before he can begin to examine God's love for him.

Whatever the reason, the best thing you can do is to keep praying for him. Also, ask a friend whose father is a Christian if his or her dad would be able to start a friendship with your dad. Sometimes adults need a person the same age so they have someone who can relate to what they're going through.

You've certainly been persistent. And you're doing exactly what this passage is talking about. You're asking, seeking, and knocking. Unfortunately, persisting in prayer will not always change the heart that is hard toward God. People have a will that can say no to any openings that God's love may try to create. Your only hope is to continue your persistent prayer. Never give up.

Will smoking and drinking keep you out of heaven?

MATTHEW 10:32–33

"Whoever acknowledges me before men, I will also acknowledge him before my Father in heaven. But whoever disowns me before men, I will disown him before my Father in heaven."

Only one thing can keep someone out of heaven: that's shutting out the Holy Spirit's reminders to repent and come back to God up until the day you die. God is not a petty God. He's not trying to keep people out on a technicality. He's completely fair and just and is fully able to judge the hearts of anyone in any culture (much better than any human).

Sin, however, has a price. Abusing your body has a price, too. Consequences will be paid. You can smoke and drink while still acknowledging Christ, yet die before your time through a drunk-driving accident or lung cancer. And it won't be God who kills you. It will be your own choices.

To me, having a good understanding of sin, repentance, and God's forgiveness is essential. It sounds like you're confused about what it takes to be a Christian. Perhaps these questions and Scriptures will shed some light:

Who has sinned? "For all have sinned and fall short of the glory of God" (Romans 3:23).

What are the consequences? "For the wages of sin is death, but the gift of God is eternal life in Christ Jesus our Lord" (Romans 6:23).

How do we get rid of sin? "But if we confess our sins to him, he can be depended on to forgive us and to cleanse us from every wrong" (1 John 1:9, TLB).

Do we have to do more than repent? "Produce fruit in keeping with repentance" (Matthew 3:8).

Does God remember our sin once we've confessed it? "I, even I, am he who blots out your transgressions, for my own sake, and remembers your sins no more" (Isaiah 43:25).

While our behavior will sometimes cause us to go through consequences we wouldn't want to face, it's our heart that God judges when it comes to heaven.

I've heard a lot about Christ and I've even prayed to him, but I'm not sure I'm ready to become a Christian.

JOHN 1:10-13

He was in the world, and though the world was made through him, the world did not recognize him. He came to that which was his own, but his own did not receive him. Yet to all who received him, to those who believed in his name, he gave the right to become children of God—children born not of natural descent, nor of human decision or a husband's will, but born of God.

Let me give you an illustration I hope you can relate to: marriage. (Okay, so you can't totally relate to it, but stick with me.)

On September 3, 1973, I met Elaine during my senior year in high school, and we started a friendship. Soon, however, I began to date someone else. At the same time, Elaine was building that friendship with me for no other reason than she liked me as a friend. When I broke up with the other girl, I started to think that Elaine might be a good girlfriend. Well, I soon found out she liked me for more than a friend (actually, she told me!). On December 14 of that year we had our first date. We dated for two years, then on December 14 of 1975, I asked her to marry me. She said yes, so we were engaged. On July 10, 1976, we said the vows that still keep us going strong today. We are now married, committed, and enjoying the benefits of being husband and wife (including two great boys).

It seems like you know a lot of facts about Christianity. But what you need to know as well as the facts is that being a Christian is a relationship with God, not just head knowledge of the facts.

The real question you have to ask yourself is, "Where am I in relation to Jesus Christ?"

Have you become acquainted with him? (Or just heard about him?) Have you started "going with him"? (Are you spending time with him?) Are you engaged to him? (Or close to being ready to make the lifetime commitment?) Or are you "married"? (Made the choice to receive his forgiveness and decide that you don't want to live life apart from him?)

It sounds to me like you're "engaged," but not really one-hundred-percent certain you're ready for the altar. That's actually a good position to be in. But eventually, you do need to decide whether you are going to give your life to him or keep it for yourself.

I didn't grow up in a Christian home. At age eighteen, when I finally realized that God wanted me to give my life to him, it was tough. I'd been in control for so long, I wasn't sure he could make my life as good as I thought I could. Let me tell you, the moment I said, "God, I don't know everything that lies ahead, but I'm going to trust you with my life," that's the moment he slowly began to show me that he could do a better job with my life than I ever could.

A Christian is someone who knows God, not just the facts on how to meet him. You've got the facts down, now you have to decide whether you want to be a follower of Jesus for the rest of your life.

I want to encourage you to make that choice soon. You'll never regret it and you just won't be able to believe what God will do with your life. He's standing at the altar waiting for you right now. I'm praying you say, "I do."

BOOKS FOR TEENS BY GREG JOHNSON

Life Is Like Driver's Ed. (Vine Books)

Man in the Making (Broadman & Holman Publishers)

WITH SUSIE SHELLENBERGER:

Lockers, Lunchlines, Chemistry, and Cliques: 77 Pretty Important Ideas on School Survival (Bethany House Publishers)

Cars, Curfews, Parties, and Parents: 77 Pretty Important Ideas on Family Survival (Bethany House Publishers)

Camp, Car Washes, Heaven, and Hell: 77 Pretty Important Ideas on Living God's Way (Bethany House Publishers)

Life, Love, Music, and Money: 77 Pretty Important Ideas on Surviving Planet Earth (Bethany House Publishers)

258 Great Dates While You Wait (Broadman & Holman Publishers)

Opening Lines: 458 Discussion Starters While You're on a Date (Broadman & Holman Publishers)

Getting Ready for the Guy/Girl Thing (Regal Books)

What Hollywood Won't Tell You About Sex, Love and Dating (Regal Books)

Keeping Your Cool While Sharing Your Faith (Tyndale House Publishers)

WITH MICHAEL ROSS:

Geek Proof Your Faith (Zondervan Publishing House)

Teen Devotionals From BHP